JAS

Gaining Spiritual Leverage

DISCOVERING THE POWER OF
PRAYER AND FASTING

Gaining Spiritual Leverage

Published by
A Church Called Home
ACCH.US

Copyright © 2024 by Jason Creech

All rights reserved.

No part of this publication may be reproduced, stored in a retrieval system, or transmitted in any form or by any means electronic, mechanical, photocopying, recording, or otherwise, without the prior written permission from the author.

All scripture quotations, unless otherwise indicated, are taken from the Holy Bible: New King James Version (NKJV), Copyright 1982.

New Spirit-Filled Life Bible, Copyright 2002 by Thomas Nelson, Inc.

ISBN: 979-8-335-09612-6

Cover Design: Jason Creech
jason@acch.us

Contents

ACKNOWLEDGEMENTS	V
INTRODUCTION	VII
1. GAINING SPIRITUAL LEVERAGE	1
2. WHAT IS BIBLICAL FASTING ALL ABOUT?	21
3. GOING FROM GOOD, TO GREAT, TO GREATER	33
4. A CHURCH ON STRIKE	51
5. PRAYER AND FASTING HEIGHTENS YOUR SENSITIVITY TO GOD'S VOICE	67
6. THE SUN STOOD STILL	89
7. WHAT TO EXPECT WHEN YOU PRAY	105
8. SOME PRAYERS EARN COMPOUND INTEREST	125
9. WHY DIDN'T GOD ANSWER MY PRAYER?	139
ANSWERED PRAYERS	145

PRAYER LIST	147
END NOTES	149
ABOUT THE AUTHOR	157
AUTHOR CONTACT	159
ADDITION RESOURCES	161

ACKNOWLEDGEMENTS

First and foremost, let me say how very thankful I am for our glorious God, His Son, and the daily inspiration of the Holy Spirit. Words could never express how grateful I am to my parents for always encouraging my brother and me to go after our dreams. My wife, Melissa, has been a champion of the faith. Her passion for Jesus inspires me and our kids. Thank you for being such an amazing wife! I know being a pastor's kid is not always easy, but our two children have made it look easy. Thank you, Tori and Chaz, for who you are.

For years, Jennifer Kitts has led the publication process of my books. I cannot thank her enough for her hard work. Thank you Karen Arnwine, Debbie Allen, and Heather Garrison for proof reading my work. Helen Wilder did the editorial work on this book, and she is an answer to prayer. Helen, I am a better writer because of you.

A special thanks to our staff, our leaders and the amazing team we have at A Church Called Home for making church so much fun.

INTRODUCTION

As a minister, one soon discovers the difference between preparing a message and receiving a word from God. I would love to say that every week I have a burning bush experience and the Holy Spirit tells me everything He wants me to say before standing on the platform He's given me. I would be lying if I told you that. There are weeks, sometimes months, in which all I do is pray, study and prepare. Then there are *those* times... I love *those* times. Those times when you know God has given you a word. That's what happened to me a few weeks ago as I drank a cup of coffee on my back porch while reading my Bible. Honestly, I was just reading through the necessary chapters for that day in my annual pursuit to read the Bible through in a year.

Then something in Amos chapter seven pinned me back in my seat. Notice the verses below:

> *Amos replied, "I'm not a professional prophet, and I was never trained to be one. I'm just a shepherd, and I take care of sycamore-fig trees. But the Lord*

called me away from my flock and told me, 'Go and prophesy to My people...'"

- Amos 7:14-15

Amos was one of what we call the Twelve Minor Prophets. But don't let the word "minor" fool you. Anytime you write something and God decides to put it in the Bible, there's nothing minor about you. Over the years, I've written a lot of material, but I've yet to write something that so impressed the Lord that He stopped print on His word to reprint using my words. Just saying!

The Twelve Minor Prophets are referred to as "minor" because the books they wrote are much shorter than the writings of those like Isaiah and Jeremiah.

The ministry of Amos took place during a time of peace and prosperity, but it was also a time of great social injustice. The rich oppressed the poor. Justice had been polluted by political corruption. A country called by God and blessed by God had forgotten its God. The theme of Amos' preaching was returning to the Lord and addressing the social injustice of the day.

Modern political and civil rights leaders have quoted Amos in their speeches. In his speech, *I Have a Dream,* Dr. Martin Luther King Jr. quoted Amos when he said, *"We will not be satisfied until justice rolls down like waters, and righteousness like a mighty stream."* That's a direct quote from Amos 5:24. Bernie Sanders referenced that same passage during his presidential campaign in 2016.

The more Amos prophesied, the more Israel's leaders grew intolerant. As Amos began to move toward the call of God on his life, opposition arose. Can you relate? If you want to see what opposition feels like, start serving in ministry. Lead a connect group in your church. Get on a ministry team. Go on a mission trip to a country where the gospel is not welcome. Chase that dream God placed in your heart. Then you'll see what opposition feels like. As Amos moved forward, friction began to take place. In the face of hostility, Amos made four powerful statements. Notice the first three:

> *"I'm not a professional prophet."*
> *"I was never trained to be one."*
> *"I'm just a shepherd."*

I wonder how long Amos wrestled with the call of God on his life. I wonder how long he allowed his excuses to keep him from his greatness. One thing I have noticed in my own life is that I cannot make progress while making excuses. Greatness begins where my excuses end.

Recently, I had a revelation about church membership. I believe people go to church for the same reason they go to the gym.

No one joins a gym to stay the same. People join a gym because they believe they can be better and feel better. People go to church for the same reason. I believe you picked this book up because you want to be better, to accomplish more, and to experience greater things. I believe God has more for you than what you've witnessed thus far. However, you cannot accomplish more while making excuses.

I wonder how long Amos allowed those three excuses to keep him from his destiny? We know what his excuses were, but what are yours? What excuses are on your list?

> *I'm too young.*
> *I'm too old.*
> *I just went through a divorce.*
> *I just lost everything I had.*
> *I tried before, it just didn't work.*
> *No one believes in me.*
> *If only I had done that differently.*

We can learn several things from Amos' story. For starters, we often believe that God is looking for better. God's not looking for someone better; He's looking for someone who's available. Realistically speaking, anything you do someone else can do better. That doesn't change the fact that God has called you, and what I know from reading Scripture is anything surrendered to Him has unlimited potential.

The text leads us to believe that Amos had some self-esteem issues. Amos had a confidence problem.

> *"I'm not a professional."*
> *"I was never trained."*
> *"I'm just a shepherd."*

There's more to you than what you see on the surface! You are not *just* anything. Humility is not the absence of confidence. Humility is when your confidence is in the Lord, not in yourself. *Christ in you is the hope of glory.*[1] My self-confidence may be low at times, but my holy confidence is off the charts.

In case you're doubting how incredible you are, let me give you something to think about. Your eye can see 10 million different colors. Your eye's retina, makes close to 10 billion calculations every second. Your heart circulates 2,000 gallons of blood through 60,000 miles of blood vessels day in and day out. Your nose can distinguish between 10,000 odors.

Your body is inhaling oxygen, metabolizing energy, maintaining equilibrium, repairing damaged tissue, purifying toxins, digesting food, and exhaling carbon dioxide. No wonder you're so tired! You deserve a nap!

Again, Amos made four powerful statements that should encourage all of us. The first three tell us a great deal about him. The last one tells us a great deal about his God. Amos said:

> *"I'm not a professional prophet."*
> *"I was never trained to be one."*
> *"I'm just a shepherd."*

Despite what Amos was not, in the face of opposition, he ends with...

> *"But the Lord called me..."*

One of my favorite words in the Bible is the word *but*. The word *but* in the Bible is like the word *void* on a check. It cancels out everything that came before it. Has anyone ever tried to apologize to you and in the middle of their apology they insert the word, *but?*

No!

No!

No!

You cannot say, "I'm sorry, *but...*"

Staring into the eyes of his critics, Amos said, "You may not think I'm qualified for this. I can give you three good reasons myself as to why I shouldn't be doing this. *But* here's what I do know - the Lord called me, and I'm not going to let anything keep me from being who He called me to be."

If you, like Amos, desire to step into the greater things God has for you, this book might add some fuel to that fire. When we pray and fast, we leverage the power of the cross to do the impossible. When we work, we work, but when we pray, God goes to work. Prayer is truly the difference between the best you can do, and the best God can do. William Booth, founder of the Salvation Army said, "Work as if everything depends on work, and pray as if everything depends on prayer."

There's an old saying, "Revivals are born after midnight." The thought behind the quote is that spiritual breakthroughs come only to those who want them badly enough. This kind of fervency demands a determined heart that will pray past the ordinary and into the extraordinary. In the words of Charles Swindoll, "Some of God's best truths, like priceless treasures, are hidden in depths most folks never take the time to search out." Job refers to God's great mysteries as, *"Things too wonderful for me, which I did not know."* [3] Daniel reminded us that the Lord, *"reveals the profound and hidden things."* [2] Paul says in Colossians 2:3, *"In Christ are hidden all the treasures of knowledge and wisdom."* There are things hidden in Christ, which like gems, one must dig out in prayer. Gaining spiritual leverage is a must for those wishing to make the most of the life God has given them.

So, if you're ready to push past mediocrity, past the average and mundane, then let's get started. Thank you for joining me.

Chapter 1
GAINING SPIRITUAL LEVERAGE

When I was a kid, my parents drove a 1973 Oldsmobile Toronado. It was nearly as long as the Empire State Building is high. That was back when you and your little brother could sleep in the rear window compartment. When we cruised down the highway, it was like riding on a cloud, floating up and down, and gently rocking side to side. That car had swag even before there was such a thing.

It was on that old Toronado that my dad taught me how to change a flat tire. He told me to remove the five lugs that held the wheel in place. Using only my fingers, I tried to unscrew the lug nuts, but it wasn't happening. It didn't take long to realize it was totally impossible in my own strength.

Then, my dad introduced me to the lug wrench tucked away in the trunk. The wrench gave me an enormous amount of leverage. What was impossible a few seconds before was more than manageable at that point. But there was one nut I could not break loose; it just wasn't going anywhere. That's when dad said, "You need a breaker bar." He went back to the trunk and returned with a pipe that was about two feet long. He told me to slide the pipe over the lug wrench and try again. It worked with ease.

Over the years, both my earthly father and my heavenly Father have taught me a great deal about gaining leverage, and that's what this book is all about. Together, we will discover how prayer and fasting create an enormous amount of spiritual leverage. Think of prayer and fasting as a giant lever; then consider what a lever does. A lever amplifies the force of input to provide a greater output. That boost of momentum is called leverage, and the longer the lever, the greater the leverage. What a lug wrench is to a lug is what prayer is to that mountain you're facing, and fasting is the breaker bar. Jesus said, *"Whatsoever you ask in prayer believing, you shall receive."* Prayer and fasting give you the spiritual leverage needed to do what you cannot do in your own strength. As we begin our journey, let's look at the following story from Mark chapter nine:

> *When they returned to the other disciples, they saw a large crowd surrounding them, and some teachers of religious law were arguing with them. 15 When the crowd saw Jesus, they were overwhelmed with awe, and they ran to greet him. 16 "What is all this arguing about?" Jesus asked. 17 One of the men in the crowd spoke up and said, "Teacher, I brought my son so you could heal him.*

He is possessed by an evil spirit that won't let him talk. 18 And whenever this spirit seizes him, it throws him violently to the ground. Then he foams at the mouth and grinds his teeth and becomes rigid. So I asked your disciples to cast out the evil spirit, but they couldn't do it."

19 Jesus said to them, "You faithless people! How long must I be with you? How long must I put up with you? Bring the boy to me." 20 So they brought the boy. But when the evil spirit saw Jesus, it threw the child into a violent convulsion, and he fell to the ground, writhing and foaming at the mouth... The boy's father said, "Have mercy on us and help us, if you can."

23 "What do you mean, 'If I can'?" Jesus asked. "Anything is possible if a person believes." 24 The father instantly cried out, "I do believe, but help me overcome my unbelief!" 25 When Jesus saw that the crowd of onlookers was growing, he rebuked the evil spirit. "Listen, you spirit that makes this boy unable to hear and speak," he said. "I command you to come out of this child and never enter him again!"

26 Then the spirit screamed and threw the boy into

another violent convulsion and left him. The boy appeared to be dead. A murmur ran through the crowd as people said, "He's dead." 27 But Jesus took him by the hand and helped him to his feet, and he stood up. 28 Afterward, when Jesus was alone in the house with his disciples, they asked him, "Why couldn't we cast out that evil spirit?" 29 And He told them, "This kind can come out by nothing but prayer and fasting.

- Mark 9:14-29

At some point in your life, you will come face to face with something you cannot handle in your own strength. At some point, you will face the impossible. You will face a mountain too high to climb, too wide to go around, and too dense to tunnel through. It might be a financial challenge. You didn't know they were going to lay off everyone in your division. You didn't know the company was in trouble and about to file bankruptcy. That business deal looked promising; you had no idea it would turn sour.

Perhaps you are facing a physical challenge; the doctors said there's nothing more they can do. It's just a matter of time. The cancer has progressed too far. They still haven't located a donor. You'll never make it through the surgery.

Maybe your mountain is a relational one, and you haven't spoken to that member of your family in over a decade. It looks as though the marriage is over. That prodigal child has gone straight up crazy, and nothing you do seems to be working.

Maybe it's a dream God put in your heart that's so big it will never get off the ground unless He steps in. Whatever the challenge may be, one thing is for sure, we all face mountains in life, and the father in Mark chapter nine was facing his Mount Everest. On his own, he was hopeless. He was facing something far beyond his expertise. All the money in the world couldn't fix it, and all the skill and know-how were not sufficient. The situation exceeded his competence. He needed a miracle.

Life is full of surprises. Life can and does surprise us, but nothing surprises God. He's never caught off guard. One thing you will never hear God say is, "Oh, my God!" Nothing surprises the Lord. However, I've lived long enough to know that life has a way of surprising us. But, in the middle of that surprise you got, God can surprise you as well.

There's no obstacle that can withstand the power of a praying child of God. Jesus had already given His disciples the power to cast out evil spirits, but they weren't getting it done in this story. What was the problem? According to Jesus, they had yet to discover the power of prayer and fasting. Some breakthroughs only come by prayer and fasting. If you are not content to go through this year the same way you went through last year, then it's time to fast and pray.

While hanging on the cross, Jesus cried out, *"It is finished!"* In other words, Jesus did everything that needed to be done so that you and I could be everything that God called us to be. He did all that was necessary so that the fullness of God's power could reside in us. Now it's up to me and you to take what Jesus did, and do something with it.

The cross has the power to change everything in your life, but, if you don't do anything with it, nothing will ever change. Prayer is leveraging the power of the cross. Prayer is making good use of the power that's available to us.

No mountain is greater than the power of prayer! That's why Jesus said in Luke 18:1, *"I wish that people would pray always and not faint."* He wasn't saying, *"I wish people would practice more religious rhetoric."* He was saying, *"I know what prayer does. There are mountains that need to be moved, seas that still need to be parted, cities to win, lives to be changed, marriages that need to be restored, and sick people who need to be healed."* Prayer is leveraging the power of the cross to do the impossible.

In September of 2012, Melissa and I embarked on our first ever church plant as lead pastors. We had never pastored a church prior to A Church Called Home. We moved to our beautiful city of Knoxville, Tennessee, only ten weeks before the first service. In hindsight, that wasn't the most brilliant thing to do, but no one has ever accused me of being brilliant. We are a part of a fellowship called ARC (Association of Related Churches). ARC has launched nearly two thousand churches across the country, many of which started with crazy numbers on their opening weekend. I would hear guys say, "We launched with 5,000 at our first service and 7,000 came to Jesus." I know that math doesn't work, and I might be exaggerating those numbers a bit, but still, I've heard some incredible stories over the years.

Those stories were not our story. We had a humble beginning. It was somewhere around week four that a man in the center of the third row had a heart attack during the second song of the worship set. We called 911; a team of paramedics came and transported him to a nearby hospital. The very next week, a woman had a severe stroke, and within minutes, she was unresponsive. We called 911, and the same paramedic team responded. One of the EMT guys looked at me in a somewhat puzzled manner and asked, "What are you doing to these people?" Without thinking, the words leaped from my mouth and I replied, "We're knocking them dead at A Church Called Home." That wasn't one of my finer moments by the way.

Three months after launch, we had a Sunday with only twenty-seven people in attendance. That's counting babies and all. Back then it was normal for the weekend offering to be $150, or less. Everything in me was screaming, "You'll never make it!" On a personal note, I was struggling to survive. As a man, you never want to admit you're failing but everything around me indicated I was. During those first three months, I spent eighteen nights without sleep, and I mean *no sleep*, not a wink. That season shed a new light on the Apostle Paul's words when he said that he was often *without sleep*.[1] Paul was a church planter. Was his lack of sleep due to long nights of passionate worship and prayer, or was Paul tossing and turning over all the "what ifs." On one of those sleepless nights, I went to pray at the theater we were leasing. That was the night I heard the Lord say to me, "Don't allow one day to define your future!"

I began to think about the difference one day can make. One day, Joseph was in prison for a crime he didn't commit; the next day he was the Vice President of Egypt. One day, Mary was just another unknown teenage girl living in obscurity, the next day she was pregnant with the Savior of the world. One day, Abram was just a rich man without any children to pass his legacy on to, the next day he was Abraham, the father of a nation and a patriarch of our faith. One day, Saul was acquiring letters to stop the church, the next day he was building the church. What a difference one day can make!

If you are suffering through today, believing God for a better someday, mark this down: your one day is on its way. However, between today and your one day, you may find yourself screaming, "Mayday, mayday!"

Oh yeah, the day after the Lord spoke all that to my heart, someone invested $13,000 into A Church Called Home and our congregation quadrupled in only a few weeks. By the following year, we had grown to roughly two hundred people. Then a friend of mine called from across town. He was on staff at a church that had recently lost its pastor. That congregation of precious people became a part of A Church Called Home, giving us a 12,000 square foot building and six acres of property. Two weeks after the property was deeded to A Church Called Home, a developer came to our office inquiring about one of the six acres. The fire department wanted to build a substation in our area, and that one acre was the ideal location. I kid you not when I say there were properties for sale all around us, but they wanted one acre of ours. We had the acre appraised and the appraisal came in at $12,000. We sold the property to the developer for $60,000. God can change a situation in just one day!

If He could use Moses to bring two million people out of bondage with nothing in his hand but a stick, what can He do in your situation? God is not limited by your current situation. Let that sink in for a moment. I said, "God is not limited by your current situation." Don't allow your current situation to overpower your heavenly position. You are seated with Christ in heavenly places, far above the struggles of this world. Believe that! Declare that! Live with that revelation. Jesus can change any situation in just one day. No one day ever defines your future.

Have you heard of a man by the name of David Wilkerson? He was the founding pastor of Times Square Church in New York City. He was called to New York in 1958 to minister to gang members and drug addicts. In 1960, he founded a faith-based organization to help teenagers, adults, and families with substance abuse problems. That organization was called Teen Challenge. In 1962, he wrote a book entitled, *The Cross and the Switchblade*.

For decades, Pastor Wilkerson's ministry offered a monthly newsletter to encourage believers around the world. In January of 1996, he shared how difficult his early days of ministry were. He wrote, "I remember awful discouragement in my early days of ministry. At times I felt overwhelmed by all the financial responsibilities. Often, I felt like a failure as a husband and father as well. I would get so low; I thought my faith would shatter completely."

In August of 2011, David Wilkerson went to be with the Lord. But what a beautiful legacy that man left behind. He didn't give up during those early days. He didn't allow the tough days to rob him of the better days. That book he wrote has sold more than 18 million copies, and it's been translated into 30 different languages. Teen Challenge has grown to over 1,200 locations operating in 118 nations, and Times Square Church is a large church in the Manhattan District where people of over 100 nationalities gather each week to worship. God can change a story in just one day! Don't let today's circumstances and yesterday's disappointments keep you from tomorrow's promises.

In his book *Soul Print*, Mark Batterson shares his own one-day story: "One of my most embarrassing ministry moments happened a few years into our church plant. I invited a band to do a concert for National Community Church. We were a church of about a hundred people at that point, and I told the band that a hundred people would show up. I was still in the naïve stage of leadership. Five minutes before that concert, the seven-member band was sitting in the green room envisioning a hundred people, and I knew there were only four people out there. I've never wanted the rapture to happen so badly! What ensued was one of the most awkward events I've ever been part of. There were more people in the band than in the audience. To top it off, one of the four people in the audience, who was a worse dancer than I am, wouldn't stop dancing."[2]

Today, National Community Church is a thriving multisite church meeting in eight different locations in and around the D.C. area, and Pastor Mark is now a New York Times Bestselling Author. During those early days when times were tough, he refused to give up. He believed that no one day ever defines our future.

Zechariah 4:10 reminds us to *not despise the day of small beginnings, for the Lord rejoices to see the work begin.* The only thing worse than a quitter is someone who never starts. There's a common denominator in every one-day story. In every one-day story, there's a child of God learning how to leverage the power of the cross through prayer.

What Jesus Did and Did Not Do

Back to the story in Mark chapter nine, let's consider what Jesus did and *did not* do in this story. For starters, His season of prayer and fasting was not reactive, but proactive.

When He encountered this situation, He didn't say to the father in the story, "I think I can help, but give Me a few days to pray and fast." In other words, He practiced a lifestyle of prayer and fasting, so when facing situations such as this one, the power of God was there to get the job done. You see, the power that's released during a season of prayer and fasting always outlives the fast itself.

At A Church Called Home, we start every year with twenty-one days of prayer and fasting. I have found that when you start your year off that way, you reap the benefits for the rest of the year. Two weeks after we concluded our fast in 2018, a friend of ours called late one night. Her dad had been in a car accident and things did not look good. He was paralyzed, on a ventilator, and totally incoherent. He was given absolutely no chance to live.

The accident was on a Monday and by Thursday, the medical staff was ready to take him off life support and let him pass. That afternoon, I met our friend and her husband at the hospital. A few of our prayer team members came to offer support as well. In the foyer of the hospital his daughter broke. Her dad was homeless, and with that lifestyle came many bad choices. She was concerned for his soul. I asked, "Before we go to see him, has he opened his eyes at all since the accident?"

GAINING SPIRITUAL LEVERAGE

She said, "No."

Then, I asked, "Has he responded in any way to anyone's voice or touch?"

Again, the answer was, "No."

As we approached the ICU, many thoughts raced through my mind. Lazarus had been dead four days when Jesus called his name. The man we were about to see was by all means dead, and he too had been in that state for four days. When Jesus sent out His disciples, He didn't tell them to pray for the sick but to *"heal the sick."* I was determined to see a miracle.

As we walked into the room, I stepped up to his side, placed my left hand on his shoulder, leaned forward and called out his name. Immediately, his eyes popped open as if he had been awakened from a deep sleep. He had been completely nonresponsive for four days; then, in an instant, he was one hundred percent present.

We communicated back and forth for several minutes. He tried to talk with the tubes still in his mouth. We established a way to communicate. To say "Yes," he would blink his eyes one time. I told him who I was and that he had been in a terrible accident. He knew things did not look good. I talked with him about the love of God and the grace of our Lord. His eyes teared up as I shared Jesus with him. I asked him if he would like to pray with me. He blinked his eyes one time to say "Yes." Together we cried out to the Lord. Right then and there, he received Jesus. A few hours later, he passed away. Our twenty-one days of prayer and fasting had proven to be proactive, not reactive. Signs and wonders followed those twenty-one days. Expect God to show up when you seek His face.

In his book, *The Circle Maker*, Mark Batterson writes, "Bold prayers honor God, and God honors bold prayers. God is not offended by your biggest dreams or boldest prayers. He is offended by anything less. If your prayers aren't impossible to you, they are insulting to God. Why? Because they don't require divine intervention. But ask God to part the Red Sea, or make the sun stand still, or float an iron ax head, and God is moved to omnipotent action."[3]

What Prayer is Not

As important as it is to understand what prayer is, it's just as important to understand what prayer is not. Prayer is not begging God to do something He doesn't want to do.

Prayer is leveraging Christ's victory over ungodly circumstances. It's carrying out on Earth, decisions already made in Heaven. What are you believing God for? What mountains are you needing to move in prayer? What ungodly situations need to change in and around you? Write these things down. Lay your hand over what you've written and call upon the Lord. Then watch God do what He does best. And

GAINING SPIRITUAL LEVERAGE

remember, prayer is like prophecy; it's the best predictor of your future. Show me how you pray, and I will show you your future.

In the book of 2 Kings, there's a beautiful story about prayer. The story revolves around King Hezekiah. He was a man who loved God, served the Lord faithfully, and at the age of twenty-five, he became King of Judah. The Bible says that the Lord was with him, and the Lord prospered all the king did. In the fourteenth year of his reign, the king of Assyria attacked all the cities of Judah. The Assyrian King sent a large army to Hezekiah's palace along with a letter. The commander of the army stood outside the palace and read the letter out loud. The letter was a death sentence threatening to destroy Hezekiah and his people. It ended with the following words:

> *Do not listen to Hezekiah, for he is misleading you when he says, 'The LORD will deliver us.' Has the god of any nation ever delivered his land from the hand of the king of Assyria?*
>
> - 2 Kings 18:33

So, how did Hezekiah respond? When all eyes were on him, 2 Kings 19:14 says, *"Hezekiah received the letter from the hand of the messengers, and read it: and Hezekiah went up into the house of the Lord and spread it before the Lord."*

What do you need to lay before the Lord right now?

Please understand that God loves everybody, but He will fight for those who belong to Him, and not everyone belongs to the Lord. The truth is, we're not born children of God. According to Ephesians 2:3, we are born *children of wrath*. I know that's not politically correct, but it is biblically correct. The Bible says in John 1:12, that we become children of God when we receive Christ as our Savior. We learn from the story of King Hezekiah, that if you get down to business with God, He will get down to business with your enemies. Your enemies will either humble themselves or God will humble them. Jesus said in Matthew 21:44, *"Whoever falls upon the Rock will be broken, but to whom the Rock falls upon, it will grind him to powder."* What does this mean? It means humble yourself before Him, or you will be humbled. Hezekiah laid that threatening letter before the Lord and prayed. The Assyrian king refused to humble himself, and that night an angel walked through the Assyrian camp and killed 185,000 soldiers. Never underestimate the power of prayer!

In the foreword of Larry Stockstill's book *The Model Man*, Pastor Chris Hodges wrote about the impact his pastor's prayer life had on him. "I came on staff at Bethany Church in January 1984 at the age of twenty. I had a passion to do ministry but knew little about it. I had five semesters of an accounting degree and was enrolled in a local Bible college, but the best education I received in ministry came from what I witnessed in Pastor Larry's leadership. For example, I didn't learn about prayer from any class. I learned by sneaking into the main auditorium of

Bethany at 4:30 a.m., on a Sunday morning to watch Pastor Larry pray. It was life changing to see him spend time with God for three hours – walking through the room putting his hands on every pew, kneeling on the stage behind the pulpit, and crying out to God for people to be saved."[4]

Make prayer a priority. Get up early and pray. Mark 1:35 says, *"Very early in the morning, while it was still dark, Jesus got up, left the house and went off to a solitary place, where He prayed."* In the Word of God, the hours between 3:00 AM and 6:00 AM are referred to as the fourth watch, and this block of time had special spiritual significance.

Jacob wrestled with the angel of the Lord during the fourth watch. Israel came out of Egyptian bondage during the fourth watch. Gideon pulled down the altars of idol worship and defeated the Midianites during the fourth watch. It was during the fourth watch that Jesus came to His disciples walking on the water. The four lepers invaded the Aramean camp and plundered their enemy during the fourth watch. It was during the fourth watch of the night that Israel defeated the Ammonites in 1 Samuel 11.

The next time you wake up during those hours, take that as an invitation to experience God in a special way. Keep a journal of the things the Holy Spirit says to you as you spend time with Him during those early morning hours.

Forbes once published an article entitled, *"Morning Time Just Became Your New Best Friend."* According to the article, love it or hate it, utilizing the morning hours before work may be the key to a successful and healthy lifestyle. That's right, early rising is a common trait found in many CEOs, government officials, and other influential people. The late British Prime Minister Margaret Thatcher was up every day at 5:00 AM, renowned architect Frank Lloyd Wright at 4:00 AM, and Robert Iger, the CEO of Disney wakes at 4:30 AM, just to name a few. I know what you're thinking: you do your best work at night. Not so fast! According to Inc. Magazine, morning people have been found to be more proactive and more productive. If you were to get up just one hour earlier each morning you would gain fifteen days in a year. Changing your schedule might just change your life.

In April of 2016, The Business Insider published an article entitled *"21 Successful People Who Wake Up Incredibly Early."* Gun Lubin and Rachel Gillett wrote, "Waking up with (or before) the sun allows executives like Apple CEO Tim Cook and *Shark Tank* investor Kevin O'Leary to get a head start on the day, knocking out tasks before the rest of the world has rolled out of bed. Those extra hours with less distractions and fresh energy, also give them a chance to do some creative thinking."

Many early risers cite increased creativity and inspiration in the morning hours. Great works of art and novels were written in the early hours of the day. If you can get up at 3:00 AM on Black Friday to save $100, you can get up at 3:00 AM for a million-dollar breakthrough. It's just a thought.

Let me challenge you to begin today to seek the Lord. Set your alarm, get up earlier than you normally do, and pray. Try it for twenty-one days. Remember, anything that does not challenge you will never change you! Allow me to offer the following advice when developing a lifestyle of prayer:

1. **Set a daily appointment.** It's those daily tweaks that lead you to the mountain peaks. Make a habit of starting your day in prayer. The truth is, more problems are solved in a prayer meeting than they are in a business meeting anyway.

2. **Set a place.** Judas knew where to find Jesus because Jesus had a certain place He loved to pray. Choose that special place. I have found that if you change your schedule and your surroundings, it might just change your life.

3. **Set a plan.** Get up, put on some worship music, get your Bible out and begin to pray. Journal what comes to your mind during that time with the Lord. Pray bold and specific prayers. What's prayed in vagueness stays in vagueness. Be specific when you pray.

4. **Set up a trophy case and celebrate answered**

prayers. It's so easy to focus on what we are believing God for and forget to celebrate what He's already done. When facing Goliath, David looked back and celebrated the victories of his past. He said, *"God delivered me from the mouth of the lion and the claw of the bear, and He will deliver this giant into my hand today."* In the back of the book, I've provided you with space to record the prayers God's already answered, the miracles that have already taken place in your life. Go ahead and start building that trophy case today.

Chapter 2
WHAT IS BIBLICAL FASTING ALL ABOUT?

The Biblical definition of fasting is going without food for a spiritual purpose. We often get creative and say we're fasting from television or social media and things such as that. There's nothing wrong with that, but let's be clear; biblical fasting is going without food for a spiritual purpose. It's not just going without food either. It's going without food *for a spiritual purpose*. Biblical fasting should always be accompanied by prayer and the study of God's Word. If I'm not spending time in prayer and the Word of God during a fast, I'm just starving myself.

There are basically three types of fasts:

1. **A partial food fast:** where you take in some foods and abstain from others.

2. **A liquid only fast:** where you drink lots of water and juices, but don't take in any solid food.

3. **An absolute fast:** where you don't eat or drink anything. This is not something you should attempt for much more than a day, and it would be wise to consult a physician before doing so.

The length of time you spend fasting is between you and the Lord. There are numerous fasts in the Word of God: one, three, seven, fourteen, twenty-one, and forty-day fasts are all found in Scripture. Daniel and Nehemiah fasted from certain foods. Daniel only ate fruits and vegetables, no meat, sweets or bread. Daniel fasted like this for twenty-one days. Nehemiah fasted several months before approaching the king.

Regardless of how long you fast, avoid making promises to the Lord as to the length of your fast. This might set you up for defeat and frustration. Whether you fast one day or forty days, if it means something to you, it means something to Him.

Think of fasting like this: if prayer is talking to God, fasting is crying out to God. Fasting is resisting something natural in order to receive something supernatural. It's saying, "no" to something you want so you can say, "yes" to something you want more. Adam lost everything by eating. He literally ate himself out of house and home. Jesus started His earthly ministry by fasting. If Jesus could not accomplish everything He needed to accomplish without fasting, what does that say about our need to fast?

GAINING SPIRITUAL LEVERAGE

Let's look at a few examples of fasting in Scripture. In 1 Samuel chapter seven, the people of Israel went on a one day fast and repented of their sin. When their enemy (the Philistines) attacked them, the Lord sent a loud thunder throughout the Philistine army. The noise confused the Philistines, they turned on themselves, and attacking one another, they fell defeated before God's people.

In Ezra 8:21, Ezra called the nation to a fast. They sought God for two things: direction and protection. The Bible says, *"They humbled themselves with fasting."* That's important because Scripture says, *"God resists the proud, but gives grace to the humble."*[1] The Lord heard their cry and answered their requests.

In 1 Kings 21, King Ahab humbled himself with fasting. He was one of the most wicked Kings to reign in Israel, but the Lord honored his fast and had mercy on the king.

Daniel did a twenty-one day fast from certain foods. He didn't eat meat, pleasant foods or the wine served from the king's table. Basically, Daniel ate fruits and vegetables, and he drank only water. Some might call that cheating since he took in some food, but remember, the day he began his fast, a war broke out in the heavens.[2] One child of God began a fast, and all of heaven responded.

Do you remember Newton's *Third Law of Motion?* For every action there's an equal and opposite reaction. Prayer is a place of action. It's the stop that gets everything started. When you pray and fast, heaven is called to action.

On the twenty-first day of Daniel's fast, he said, *"Suddenly a hand touched me, my knees buckled, and my hands shook."[3]* Are you ready for a suddenly moment? Do you need a touch from God? That's what happens when you pray and fast.

In Acts 13:1-4, during a fast Paul and Barnabas were given clear instructions as to their next ministry assignment. Fasting increased their spiritual clarity. Their fast actually "*ministered to the Lord*." We also see in Scripture that the early church fasted before making major decisions.[4]

Acts chapter ten tells the story of a man by the name of Cornelius, who gave himself to prayer. He was four days into a fast when he and those with him received the baptism of the Holy Spirit. One man's desperate heart for God was the breaker bar for all those around him. The Holy Spirit came upon the Gentiles (non-Jewish people) as a result of one man's season of fasting. If you're not a Jew, you're a Gentile. Every encounter you've ever had with the Holy Spirit links back to a man named Cornelius and the fourth day of his fast.

I'm going to prophesy something over you right now. Just as Cornelius' fast reached beyond his generation, the breakthroughs you will experience during your fast will impact generations to come. People you may never meet in this lifetime will benefit from the time you're spending with the Father right now.

From 1775 to 1784, during the American revolution, Congress issued sixteen separate spiritual proclamations, calling the American people to humble themselves, fast, pray, and give thanks to God. On June 12, 1775, the Continental Congress issued one of the first proclamations when John Hancock was president of Congress. Hancock, was the son and grandson of Christian ministers, and was personally a deeply committed Christian. Sixteen such proclamations were issued by Congress asking states to observe the Christian practice of prayer and fasting. They petitioned Heaven praying that God's favor might be secured in America's bid for freedom. America was birthed by prayer and fasting.

We live in a gluttonous society. When I was ordained, my pastor told me that REV. was not short for reverend, but actually an acronym for *Rest*, *Eat* and *Visit*. That's too funny! On a more serious note, do you know why judgment came upon Sodom and Gomorrah? I used to think it was because of their homosexual lifestyle. However, look at what Scripture says in Ezekiel chapter sixteen:

> *Look, this was the iniquity of your sister Sodom: She and her daughter had pride, fullness of food, and abundance of idleness; neither did she*

strengthen the hand of the poor and needy. 50 And they were haughty and committed abomination before Me; therefore, I took them away as I saw fit.
- Ezekiel 16:49-50

Their sin consisted of pride, gluttony, laziness, greed, arrogance and sexual immorality. Gluttony was number two on the list. In 2006, Procter and Gamble said that our country could have solved world hunger using just the sum of money spent that year on ice-cream alone. As Americans, we make up less than 5% of the world's population but consume over 25% of its resources. Americans eat 815 billion calories of food each day. That's roughly 200 billion more than needed. Keep in mind 25,000 people die globally each day from starvation. Americans throw out 200,000 tons of edible food daily. The average American generates 52 tons of garbage by age 75.[5]

I'll admit I have a great love for food. In my teens and early twenties, I couldn't gain weight to save my life. Then somewhere around age twenty-seven the fast food and cheesecake caught up with me. One morning I woke up looking like the Pillsbury Doughboy. Over the years, I've shed weight, then put it back on. I hate to diet, partly because the first three letters of the word spell *die*.

Our pets are a testimony to my food obsession. We had a black Lab named Puddin, two cats named Waffles and Pancakes, who were from the same litter, and a rescue cat named Bagels. Have I mentioned I hate cats? It's obvious, the only thing we love more than pets is food. One morning while getting dressed, my wife came in our bedroom. As I stood there shirtless, she said, "You know, we should start going to the gym." Since I was the only one in the room with my shirt off and she's 117 pounds of pure gorgeous, I got the hint.

The first time I began studying the topic of fasting was when I read a book by Pastor Jentezen Franklin. There I was, eating a bag of mini chocolate donuts, drinking a large sweet tea, while reading a book entitled, *Fasting*. After reading the first three pages I thought to myself, "This isn't right. I can't eat these donuts and read this book at the same time." So, I tossed the book aside and finished my donuts. True story! I've also been known to hide chips in undisclosed locations and sneak a handful when a certain lady in my house wasn't looking. Don't judge me!

Being saved in a Pentecostal Church, one of the verses we loved to quote was Joel 2:28. The passage reads, *"And it shall come to pass afterward that I will pour out My Spirit on all flesh; your sons and your daughters shall prophesy, your old men shall dream dreams, your young men shall see visions."*

That's a powerful piece of Scripture. But notice the first part of the verse, *"And it shall come to pass afterward..."*

After what?

Good question.

Let's look back at verse twelve.

> *"Now, therefore," says the Lord, "Turn to Me with all your heart, with fasting, with weeping, and with mourning."*
>
> - Joel 2:12

God always responds to our hunger for Him. Jesus said, "*Blessed are those who hunger and thirst after righteousness, they shall be filled...*"[6] *In* Jeremiah 33:3, God said, "*Call on Me and I will answer you, and show you great and mighty things that you know not of.*" We talk a lot about revival; let's talk about *previval,* the things that precede a move of God. Throughout history, when the level of desperation rises within the church, and people begin to seek the Lord, God shows up, and unexplainable things happen. Prayer and fasting spark the fire of revival. Abraham Lincoln once said, "Give me six hours to chop down a tree, and I'll spend the first four sharpening the axe."[7] If you want that tree to come down, you better sharpen that axe. If you want to see God move, you'd better learn to pray.

The history of the church is a history of prayer. When it comes to famous preachers throughout times past, Charles Spurgeon scores high on the list. Spurgeon once stated, "Whenever God determines to do a great work, He first sets His people to pray."

Spurgeon said that neither his sermons, nor his good works accounted for the spiritual impact of his ministry. Instead, it was, as one writer put it, "The prayers of an illiterate lay brother who sat on the pulpit steps pleading for the success of the sermon." It was Spurgeon's partnership with praying people that made his ministry effective. Prayer makes an ordinary man an extraordinary man.

The year was 1949 when evangelist Billy Graham held an extended campaign that resulted in a change of approach in reaching people with the gospel. This new approach ushered in an era of mass evangelism that continues to this day. Graham confessed that he had conducted many similar events with much less impact. He concluded that the only difference between that crusade and all those before it, was the amount of prayer that he and his team invested.

John Maxwell is a name greatly associated with leadership both in and beyond the church. Yet, behind his many resources and speaking engagements, he is a man devoted to prayer. In his book *Partners in Prayer*, Maxwell writes about an experience he had at a church he pastored in San Diego, California. In his first week as pastor, a man named Bill Klassen made an appointment to meet on a Monday morning. After the two prayed together, Bill went home and told his wife that he had met the man he was proud to call *pastor*. He said, "I haven't heard him preach, but I've heard him pray."

Years later Maxwell would write, "Prayer has become an inseparable part of my life and the reason for any success I've achieved. Every major milestone of growth I've experienced has come as the result of God touching me during times of prayer. I believe those milestones never would have happened, had I not been spending regular times alone with God. Since 1972, rarely has a week gone by when I haven't awakened at least once between two and three o'clock in the morning. Each time, if I can't fall back to sleep within fifteen minutes, I assume God wants to speak to me, and I get out of bed and go to my office downstairs. I get out a pen, legal pad, and Bible, and I spend the remaining hours of the night with Him."[8]

I'm reminded of a story I once heard about a group of climbers who tried twice to reach the top of Mount Everest. Two of their team members died in the attempt. They met in London a few weeks later to give a report to their supporters. The backdrop of the stage was a large picture of Everest. One of the climbers stood to speak. Pointing at the picture he said, "You have conquered us once, you have conquered us twice, but Mount Everest; you will not conquer us again. You know why Everest? Because you cannot get any bigger; you cannot grow any longer, but we can."

Understand that as we pray and fast, we grow to meet the challenges we face. Prayer and fasting increases our spiritual capacity. Those two things are truly the difference between an ordinary Christian life and an extraordinary Christian life.

In his book, *Never Give Up*, John Mason writes, "I often hear people say, 'I'd give anything to be able to...' If you've said this, you should adopt the *6x1=6 Principle*. If you want to write a book, learn to play a musical instrument, become a better tennis player, or anything else that's important to you, then devote yourself to it one hour a day, six days a week. Sooner than you think, your desire will become a reality. You can accomplish many things in 312 hours a year! Just a commitment of one hour a day, six days a week, is all it takes. Psalm 90:12 says, '*So teach me to number my days, that I may apply my heart unto wisdom.*'" This same principle applies to our spiritual dreams as well. Great moves of God are waiting to become a reality. If we will seek His face, He will not disappoint.

To Settle or To Soar

In Matthew chapter four, we find what is referred to as the temptation of Christ. Jesus was on a forty-day fast before starting His earthly ministry. During His fast, the Bible says that He was tempted by the devil, but think about how the temptation started. The devil said, "*If You are the Son of God, command these stones to become bread.*"

You call that a temptation?

What's wrong with turning stones to bread?

If I was Jesus and my arch enemy laid a challenge on me like that, I would have snapped my fingers, and every rock in the desert would have become bread: wheat bread, white bread, sour dough bread, rye bread, multigrain bread, raisin bread, gluten free bread, flat bread, bread sticks, cheesy bread, cornbread, Mexican cornbread, you get the picture!

What's so wrong with turning stones to bread?

That's just it. The temptation wasn't to sin, but to settle - to settle for a life short of the power that only comes by prayer and fasting. Scripture says that Jesus went into the wilderness being "*led by the Spirit*," but after fasting, He returned "*in the power of the Spirit*." Angels ministered to Him at the end of His fast, demons came out of people, the sick were healed, the lame walked, and His fame traveled far and wide.

We know what happened on the other side of Jesus' fast, but you don't know what might happen on the other side of yours. Take a moment to contemplate what could take place on the other side of your season of prayer and fasting. Write those possibilities below.

Chapter 3
GOING FROM GOOD, TO GREAT, TO GREATER

According to an article in *US News*, Americans spend over $60 billion each year on weight loss fads. I can save you some money and tell you how to lose twenty pounds or more this year – FAST!

Seriously though, let me share a few thoughts to help you get your mind around how much $60 billion really is:

- Our nation's free and reduced lunch program spends nearly $11 billion each year feeding children from low income homes.

- Last year the United States gave $13 billion in humanitarian assistance worldwide. According to UN Secretary-General Antonio Guterres, global humanitarian needs are at a record high. More than 1% of the world's population are displaced from their homes and 260 million people face a food crisis. The reasons have not changed: unresolved conflicts continue while new wars are launched, leaving ordinary people to pay an unacceptable price.

You could underwrite our country's free and reduced lunch program and humanitarian aid budget and still not spend half of what we spent last year on weight loss fads alone. Lord, have mercy on us!

We all know there are two things that are guaranteed to help us lose weight, and they don't cost us anything. What are they? Exercise more and eat less. However, we will do everything else except these two things hoping to look better. I hate to break the news to you, but the only way to be better is to do better.

What we do in the natural, we do in the spiritual. We all have areas in our lives in which we desperately need a God-sized breakthrough, something only God can do. Yet for some reason we will do everything except pray and fast. These two things don't cost us a dime; yet they're the two things we neglect the most. There is a shortcut to your breakthrough, but it's uphill all the way. Anything worth anything is an uphill climb, but prayer, joined with a season of fasting, is like riding an escalator. Life is still uphill, but there's something underneath you, propelling you to the top. Today I want to show you a simple principle that will take you to another level this year.

In Mark chapter four, Jesus shares what we call *The Parable of the Sower*. He compares the word of God to seed, and our hearts to soil. In the parable, He mentions four types of soil. In verse twenty He says, "*But these are the ones sown on good ground, those who hear the word, accept it, and bear fruit: some thirtyfold, some sixty, and some a hundred.*"

Notice what Jesus is saying in this passage. Some of His children bring forth a thirtyfold return, some sixty, and some one hundred. In other words, some produce a lot more than others. The question is, "What's the difference maker?" You see, I want to live at my full potential, so how do I get a one hundred fold return on what's been invested? In Matthew six, Jesus taught on three spiritual disciplines, and I believe these three disciplines are the difference makers. These three disciplines are: giving, praying, and fasting. Let's study each one.

Giving

> *So when you give, do not announce it with trumpets, as the hypocrites do in the synagogues and on the streets, to be honored by others. Truly I tell you, they have received their reward in full. But when you give, do not let your left hand know what your right hand is doing, 4 so that your giving may be in secret. Then your Father, who sees what is done in secret, will reward you openly.* – Matthew 6:2-4

Notice that Jesus didn't say, "*If you give,*" but, "*when you give.*" God is a giver, and if He lives in you, giving is a part of your spiritual DNA. We see from this passage that giving is a private discipline that yields a public reward. If you want to be a thirtyfold person, be a generous person - give, tithe, and sow into God's kingdom. There are some who say that they can't afford to give. The truth is, you can't afford not to give. Your bank statement is also your faith statement. There are 500 verses in the Bible on prayer and 500 on faith, so these two subjects are extremely important to God. However, there are 2,350 verses on the topic of money. Fifteen percent of the Bible is about money and material wealth. God cares about how we manage our finances.

We must remember that what we have is a gift from God. Our talents, our minds, our ability to make money, are all gifts from our Creator. Every blessing we don't turn back into praise will eventually turn into pride.

People say, "If I had more money I would give more." That's not true. If you don't give now, you wouldn't give then. Giving is an act of discipline and priority. What you do with $100 reveals what you would do if you had $1 million. If you waste $100, you will waste $1 million. John D. Rockefeller once said, "I never would have been able to tithe the first million dollars I ever made if I had not tithed my first salary, which was $1.50 per week."

We cannot forget that God multiplies by subtraction. Give, and it will come back to you.[1] It's the principle of sowing and reaping. You can only reap off what you've sown. If what you have is not enough to meet your need, make it a seed. You cannot keep the seed in your hand and expect a harvest. It has to leave your hand. Once you've planted it, be confident that what was sown away was not thrown away. It's coming back! Just the other day, I heard someone say, "You cannot have uphill hopes while maintaining downhill habits." Tithing is an uphill habit that promises uphill hopes.

Several years ago, I began asking myself, "Is tithing a New Testament principle?" I know tithing is biblical, but is it something directly connected to the Law of Moses that we are not required to do on this side of the cross?

Melissa and I tithe. We love investing in the local church, and tithing has never been something we wanted to "get out of." However, the question still remained, "Is tithing a New Testament requirement?" One day, I was discussing the question with a friend. He said, "Imagine that you invited my family over to your house for dinner one evening. Our families live five hours apart, and on the set day, we drive the distance to spend some quality time with one another. I ring the doorbell, and you answer with a smile. The food is already prepared, and the aroma fills the house. All my favorites are on the table. Then what if you said, 'Guys, we are so glad you drove all this way to join us. If you don't mind, have a seat in the living room. My family and I will eat first, and when we finish, you can have what's left over.'"

Then my friend said, "Jason, tithing is not about the law; it's about honor. If you did that to my family, would you be honoring us? Of course not! But, isn't that how many of us treat the Lord with our finances? Tithing is a matter of honor, and if it's not the first thing you do with what you have, it's still not honoring to God." I will never forget that conversation. Now I give, not because I feel I *have to*, but because I *love to*. Let me also add that tithing is not the goal, it's the starting point. When James Cash Penney, otherwise known as J.C. Penney, was a young business man, he tithed ten percent of his income and lived off ninety percent. By the time he reached the end of his life, he was giving ninety percent and living off ten percent. If you really want to know how I'm doing spiritually, all you have to do is look at my checkbook. It doesn't lie. It doesn't just reveal how I'm doing financially; it reveals how I'm doing spiritually.

God is a giver; He gave His son. Jesus is a giver; He gave His life for us. The Holy Spirit is a giver; He brought us nine spiritual gifts. Everything about our God screams generosity. If we belong to Him, giving is simply a part of our spiritual DNA.

Do you know where the word worship first appears in the Bible? Do you remember what was taking place? I'll give you a hint. No one was singing. No one was playing an instrument. There was a man and his sacrifice climbing a mountain. Abraham trudging up a hillside with his son Isaac on his way to offer to the Lord the one thing dearest to his heart, and he called that *worship*. Worship always costs us something! Great worship carries with it a great price.

There's a simple way to gauge the spiritual condition of our hearts. We can do so by asking ourselves, "How do I spend my time, and how do I spend my money?" Luke 12:34 says, "*For where your treasure is, there will your heart be also."* Where your money goes is where your heart goes. Money is neither good nor bad, but the way we use it reveals what we love.

All the wealth of this world belongs to God. Haggai 2:8 says, "*The silver is mine, and the gold is mine, says the Lord of hosts.*" In his article *How We Spend Reveals Who We Are*, Pastor Arnold Martin writes, "If most Christians were executives in some corporation and handled the company's money like they handle God's money, they would be in jail for embezzlement."

I have a friend who says that he was so poor growing up that his Cheerios were just o's – there wasn't anything cheery about them. But my friend learned to honor God with what he had, he learned that God can do more with a little than we can do with a lot.

In his book, *All In*, Mark Batterson writes, "Let me be blunt, because on the subject of money, Jesus was. Obedience can be measured in dollars and cents. So, can faith. It's certainly not the only measure, but it's one of the most accurate. If we give God two percent of our income, can we really say we are one hundred percent committed to Him and His cause? I think not. If we withhold the tithe, can we really say, 'In God we trust?' If we give God our leftovers instead of our first fruits, can we really say we're seeking first His kingdom? God doesn't need our money, but He does want our hearts, and where your money is, there your heart will be also."[2]

God wants to bless you! The truth is He already has. I just finished reading a book by Art Rainer entitled, *The Money Challenge*. It's one of the best books I've read on stewardship. He writes, "All of us are susceptible to comparison. We compare what we have with what others have. But those with whom we compare ourselves tend to be relatively few, and they also tend to be those who have more than we do. This small wealthier pool of individuals warps the way we view ourselves. We begin to think we are lacking in resources. But are we?

There's a website called globalrichlist.com. This site allows you to type in your income or total wealth and compare it to that of others around the world. The results may surprise you. Did you know if someone takes home $25,000 in a year, they are in the top 2% of the world's wealthiest? This means that 98% of the world's population makes less than $25,000 a year."

You and I are blessed. As God continues to bless us, He trusts that we will be a blessing. The question is, "If He gets it to you, can He get it through you?"

I have a friend who's not the greatest steward of his resources. He once told me that several creditors were calling him, and one was relentless. One day he answered the phone and told the persistent debt collector, "Here's how this is going to work. You are one of six creditors I owe money to. I get paid every Friday, and every Friday I write each company's name on a piece of paper. I fold each piece into a tiny square and put them in a hat. I shake the hat, pull out a piece of paper, unfold it, and that's who I pay that week. If you call me one more time, I'm taking your name out of my hat!"

That's too funny!

The truth is, my friend isn't the only one in a financial mess. Last year, banks in the United States took in over $11 billion in overdraft fees. That's an unfathomable amount for most people. If you made one dollar every second for the rest of your life, it would take you 350 years to make that amount of money. Imagine what God could do if we simply gave Him what we gave the bank in overdraft fees. Seriously!

Please understand that God wants you blessed. Look at the following verses:

> *Do not fear, little flock, for it is your Father's good pleasure to give you the kingdom.*
> - Luke 12:32

> *He who did not spare His own Son, but delivered Him up for us all, how shall He not with Him also freely give us all things?*
> - Romans 8:32

The blessing of the Lord makes one rich, and He adds no sorrow with it.

- Proverbs 10:22

Now, it's also important to understand why God wants to bless us. He wants to bless us so we can be a blessing. According to finance guru, Dave Ramsey, only 2.7% of Christians in America tithe, yet 17% of Americans say they tithe. That's rather funny! If I'm not mistaken, there was a couple who died in the book of Acts because they lied about their giving, but let's not go there! A whopping 37% of people who go to church every week do not give anything to the church they attend. If I'm really a Christ follower, how could I enjoy God's house and choke His bride at the same time?

Tithing predates the law by four hundred and fifty years; before the Law of Moses, Abraham gave a tithe. Remember Abraham was the father of our faith; Moses was the father of the law. Tithing postdates the law as well. Speaking of tithing, Jesus said, "...*this you should have done...*"[4]

Twenty-two times in the book of Proverbs, the wisest man who ever lived (outside of Christ) referred to the tithe as a first-fruit offering. In other words, it's the first thing we do with our income. God is first whether you put Him there or not, you cannot rearrange the universe. Before the universe was, God was. When I tithe, I acknowledge the fact that God is first. We put Him first because He is first. The Hebrew word for tithe is MAASER (mah-as-ayr). The Hebrew word for rich is ASER (aw-shar'). There's a blessing in the tithe.

If you want to be a thirtyfold believer, be generous. Give and give cheerfully. God is a giver, and you cannot out give Him. What you sow away, you never throw away. It's coming back!

Praying

> *And when you pray, you shall not be like the hypocrites. For they love to pray standing in the synagogues and on the corners of the streets, that they may be seen by men. Assuredly, I say to you, they have their reward. 6 But you, when you pray, go into your room, and when you have shut your door, pray to your Father who is in the secret place; and your Father who sees in secret will reward you openly.*
>
> - Matthew 6:5-6

Once again, He didn't say, *"If you pray,"* but, *"When you pray."* Prayer is a private discipline that yields a public reward. If you want to be a sixtyfold person, pray. Seek God!

As I mentioned earlier, our church begins each year with twenty-one days of corporate prayer and fasting. This past year, there were certain things I had been asking the Lord for. As I was praying about one of those things, I felt a cloud of guilt come over me. In the back of my head, there was a little voice saying, "Why do you bother the Lord with all your requests? You are so needy. You are so ungrateful. A grateful man would be content with what he already has." Perhaps you've battled thoughts like that as well.

Then I had a revelation. What if I woke my kids up on Christmas Morning and said, "It's Christmas! It's time to gather around the tree!" What if my kids said, "Dad, we really don't want what's under that tree. We're just not interested in what you have for us." That would break my heart, right? Listen, Jesus paid a great price for the things He's provided for you and me. When we pray, we are like children rushing to the tree on Christmas Morning. Your request is never a bother to the Lord. That's why Proverbs 15:8 says, "*The Lord delights in the prayers of His people.*"

Prayer is a catalyst for miracles. Peter Wagner once said, "God has made certain things He wishes to do in human affairs contingent on the prayers of His people." He has willifully put Himself in partnership with His Church, and there are certain things He will not do until His Church begins to pray. In her book, *Miracles Happen When You Pray*, Quin Sherrer shares the following on the power of prayer.

"When Marine Major General Charles Krulak needed a miracle of water for troops about to lead an attack on Iraq during the

1991 war in the Persian Gulf, he did what he always did: he prayed.

He had been assigned to prepare supplies for the frontal attack by allied forces against Iraqi troops. Because of the threat of chemical warfare, lots of water would be needed for the decontamination process.

He thought he was ready, having dug water wells that could supply one hundred thousand gallons a day for the ground offensive. Then General Norman Schwarzkopf's strategy changed as the Iraqis dug in. General Krulak's operation was to move to a flat area called 'gravel plains,' seventy-four miles to the northwest.

As they dug for water there, only desert dust came out. The general consulted oil company engineers and Saudi Bedouins; still no water – only dry holes.

General Krulak prayed every day for a solution to the water problem as well as for the war effort. Ever since 1977 he had made it his practice to pray at 7:15 each morning. Staff members were invited to join him. The anticipated ground attack was only a few days away. One morning a colonel interrupted their prayer meeting to ask the general to accompany him somewhere. He had discovered something, but he would not say what. He wanted the general to see for himself.

As they traveled down a road built by the Marine Corps, they saw what looked like a pipe sticking out of the ground about fifty meters off the road. A bar protruding from the pipe formed a cross. Then the general saw at the base of the pipe a newly painted red pump, a green diesel generator, four new batteries still wrapped in plastic, and one thousand gallons of diesel fuel stored in a tank above the ground.

All the equipment was new, and everything seemed ready to operate – except there was no key to start the generator. The general looked at his officer and said, 'God did not put this here for us to be defeated for lack of a key.'

Amazingly, when General Krulak pushed the starter, the new German-made generator purred like a kitten and water began to flow. The well flowed within ten gallons of the one hundred thousand a day needed for the assault.

The general had traveled down that road many times, as had a division of men, some twenty-thousand troops. No one had reported seeing that pipe. General Krulak believes the well appeared as an answer to prayer. 'There was no way anyone could have driven down that road and not seen that well and equipment painted in multiple colors. I believe the Lord provided fuel we did not have,' he said.

With the water problem solved, military experts still predicted heavy casualties. Krulak believes God performed yet another miracle in answer to prayer. On February 24, just fifteen minutes before the 4 AM ground attack, the wind shifted, blowing from southwest to northeast. 'Winds always blow in the same direction in that part of the country,' Krulak said. This change of wind neutralized the threat of poison gas, which now would have blown back toward the Iraqis. The wind changed back to its normal direction on February 28, within minutes of General Schwarzkopf's cease-fire order. 'That,' declares Krulak, now the Commandant of the US Marine Corps, 'is the power of prayer.'"[5]

Prayer is the difference between your best and God's best. If you want to be sixty times greater than you are right now, learn to pray. When you win in prayer, you win everywhere.

Fasting

> *Moreover, when you fast, do not be like the hypocrites, with a sad countenance. For they disfigure their faces that they may appear to men to be fasting. Assuredly, I say to you, they have their reward. 17 But you, when you fast pray, anoint your head and wash your face, 18 so that you do not appear to men to be fasting, but to your Father who is in the secret place; and your Father who sees in secret will reward you openly.*
>
> - Matthew 6:16-18

Prayer and fasting is like nitro meets glycerin; together they become a spiritual weapon of mass destruction. I believe fasting is the difference between a sixtyfold child of God and a hundredfold child of God. When your hunger for God exceeds your hunger for food, great things begin to happen. Breakthroughs come like never before when you pray and fast.

When our son Chaz was four years old, he was diagnosed with autism. Along with autism comes a range of sensory issues. He could not tolerate having his teeth brushed, his hair combed, or his nails trimmed, and going to the potty was out of the question. If you set him on the commode, he would go wild. His mother and I felt totally alone and totally helpless. Our hearts broke for our son, and we were desperate.

A common issue in autistic children is a variety of gastro-intestinal issues. For the first six years of Chaz's life, he struggled severely in this area. Out of respect for my son, I will leave it at that.

One day, during a staff meeting at our church, I broke down. Six years of pain and confusion came out in a flood of emotions. A few hours later, our pastor came to me and said, "Tomorrow, I'm beginning a seven day fast for Chaz." Until that time, I knew very little about fasting. I knew Jesus fasted for forty days at the beginning of His ministry, and that He taught His disciples to fast when confronting certain challenges. However, I had never considered fasting a necessary discipline. But if my pastor was going to fast for my son, you better believe I was going to as well.

For seven days, I took in nothing but liquids. The first two days were hell on earth, but on the third day, my craving for food faded, my mind seemed clearer than ever, and prayer was sweeter than words could express. I was in a zone.

On the seventh day, I was walking down the hallway of our home. As I passed the bathroom, a foul odor nearly knocked me to the floor. I leaned close to the door, covering my nose, and asked, "Who's in there?"

Just as calm as ever, Chaz said, "It's me, daddy."

"What are you doing, son?" I asked.

He said, "I'm plop plopping."

He was six years old, and he had never used the potty a day in his life – not even once! On the seventh day of that fast, everything changed! We had a breakthrough, and he never looked back! The GI issues were gone! The sensory issues were gone! God did a miracle in our son's life, a miracle only He could have done.

Chaz's performance at school improved that year also. When we took him back to the University of Louisville for reevaluation, the staff said that he didn't seem like the same kid. Chaz graduated from high school with honors and he's currently finishing his bachelor's degree at the University of Tennessee. He's a hard-working student with a bright future ahead of him. God delivered our son!

The year he was diagnosed, his pediatrician told us that if he was lucky, he might get to sit in a regular kindergarten classroom. The devil is a liar! Don't let yesterday's disappointments keep you from today's promises! Seek the Lord. That mountain you're facing will move!

Chapter 4
A CHURCH ON STRIKE

In 1997, 185,000 UPS employees went on strike. It was the largest corporate strike of the 1990's. Those on strike were insisting on full-time jobs rather than part-time, along with increased wages. The employees gained major support from the public and eventually, their demands were met. The strike cost the company over $600 million in business. Nothing demands change more than a strike.

During the late 1950's, the steel industry was booming. As profits skyrocketed, steel workers grew more and more frustrated. Management had been working hard to remove a contract clause that favored employees. In 1959, over 500,000 union workers went on strike. The union got what the members wanted, and changes were made. Nothing demands change more than a strike.

In March of 1970, over 210,000 postal workers joined their voices and went on strike. Low wages and poor working conditions were no longer acceptable. These federal employees stood in defiance of our government and demanded change.

President Nixon had to call upon the National Guard to distribute mail during the eight-day strike. The strike influenced the signing of the Postal Reorganization Act of 1970 which completely transformed the postal business. On July 1, 1971, five federal postal unions merged to form the American Postal Workers Union, which is the largest postal union in the world. Nothing demands change more than a strike.

When a group of people go on strike, they do so for one reason: to redefine what *is* and *is not* acceptable. When enough people determine that their situation is no longer acceptable, they pull together and strike. Their actions create leverage, and that leverage creates change.

Fasting is going on a hunger strike to demand spiritual breakthrough. When we fast, we're not demanding God to change our situation; we're demanding our situation to line up with the Word of God. When a church comes together for a corporate fast, that congregation of believers unites their voices to oppose Hell, and to demand spiritual breakthrough. As a result, change happens! The gates of Hell will not prevail.

When Queen Esther discovered Haman's plot to kill her people, she called the entire Hebrew nation to a three day fast. Genocide was not acceptable to the Queen. She and her people were not going to sit idle and watch their enemy have his way. They cried out to God and demanded that situation to change, and change it did! Haman's plot was exposed, and the King of Persia ordered that he be hung from the very gallows he had built for Esther's people.

If you knew your breakthrough was only three days away, wouldn't you fast?

One of my favorite chapters in Scripture is 2 Samuel 23. The chapter is a testimony of King David's life and a summary of God's covenant with the house of David. Starting at verse eight, we read about David's top three warriors, his men of valor.

The first one was a man who went by the name Adino the Eznite. In one battle, he killed eight hundred men with only one spear. Why? Because those men were trying to take possession of the land that belonged to him and his people, and to Adino the Eznite, that was not acceptable.

The second man was Eleazar. When the armies of Israel fled during battle, Eleazar and David stood their ground and refused to retreat. Eleazar fought so fiercely that his hand literally drew up around his sword. After the battle ended, no one could separate the sword from his hand. Why did he fight so fiercely? Because retreating in battle was not acceptable to Eleazar.

The third warrior was Shammah who stood alone in the middle of a field defending what God had given his people. When the Philistines attacked, he boldly fought until his enemies were defeated. Why? Because losing his property was not acceptable to Shammah.

Each of these stories ends with, *"And the Lord brought about a great victory that day."* God is so ready to come to your aid right now. He is on the edge of His throne waiting to move on your behalf. He is just waiting for you and I to say, "Enough is enough! I'll fight off eight hundred devils if need be. I'll swing that sword until my arm falls off. I'm ready to fight for what God has promised me!" What are you willing to fight for today? As you move into a season of prayer and fasting, define what you are fighting for. Remember, what's prayed in vagueness stays in vagueness. Be specific.

Romans 16:20 is a verse that used to bother me. The passage reads, *"And the God of peace will soon crush Satan underneath your feet."* That *"soon"* word bothered me for years. My question was, *"How soon?"* The answer is *"as soon as you begin to pray!"* When we pray, we enforce the victory won at the cross. As soon as you pray, your victory is on its way. God will do for you what He did for those three guys in 2 Samuel 23. But it all starts with redefining what *is* and *is not* acceptable. Someone once said, "You can do more after you pray, but you cannot do more until you pray." Prayer is the winning blow, it's the knockout punch, work is just gathering up the results.

There's actually a simple quiz you can take to determine whether or not it's time for a season of fasting. If you answer *yes* to any of the following questions, it's time to go on strike.

- Are you or someone you love in need of healing?

- Do you need the touch of God in a specific area of your life?

- Is there a dream inside of you that only God can make possible?

- Are you in need of a fresh encounter with the Lord?

- Do you desire a heightened sensitivity to the voice of God?

- Do you need to overcome some form of bondage or addiction?

- Do you need God's direction on an important decision?

- Is there a friend or loved one who needs to be saved?

If any situation in your life is going to change, it begins with redefining what *is* and *is not* acceptable. Let me give you an example: I would like to weigh 180 pounds again, so I started this year with a goal of losing twenty pounds. That was four months ago, and I only have thirty-five pounds to go. You see, as long as peanut butter fudge and potato chips are acceptable midnight snacks, my weight is not going to change. Change only comes when you redefine what *is* and *is not* acceptable.

Suddenly

There's a word that appears seventy times in the Bible and the context in which it appears messes with me. The word is *suddenly*. Here's why it messes with me. When I read the stories in which the word appears, it seems to me the word *finally* would be a better choice of words. Suddenly just doesn't seem to fit. Let me show you what I mean. Look at what Daniel said on the twenty-first day of his fast.

> *Suddenly, a hand touched me, which made me tremble on my knees and on the palms of my hands. 11 And He said to me, "O Daniel, man greatly beloved, understand the words that I speak to you, and stand upright, for I have now been sent to you." While he was speaking this word to me, I stood trembling.*
>
> - Daniel 10:10-11

Twenty-one days without food sounds more like *finally* than *suddenly*. In every strike, there's a moment of breakthrough, a moment of change, a *suddenly* moment. Now think about what happened on the Day of Pentecost. One hundred and twenty people were huddled in a room seeking the Lord for ten days. On the tenth day, the Bible says, "*When the Day of Pentecost had fully come; they were all with one accord in one place.*[1] *And suddenly there came a sound from heaven, as of a rushing mighty wind, and it filled the whole house where they were sitting."* These people had been in non-stop worship and prayer for ten days straight. The Prophet Joel prophesied this event 850 years before it happened. Doesn't that sound more like a *finally* than a *suddenly* to you?

What about the story of Paul and Silas in prison? In the sixteenth chapter of Acts, Paul and Silas were preaching Jesus, and a woman tormented by an evil spirit was set free. They didn't get an honorarium for preaching; they were thrown in prison for preaching. Notice how Scripture records the event:

> *And they brought them to the magistrates, and said, "These men, being Jews, exceedingly trouble our city; 21 and they teach customs which are not lawful for us, being Romans, to receive or observe." 22 Then the multitude rose up together against them; and the magistrates tore off their clothes and commanded them to be beaten with rods. 23 And when they had laid many stripes on them, they threw them into prison, commanding the jailer to keep them securely. 24 Having received such a charge, he put them into the inner prison and fastened their feet in the stocks. 25 But at midnight Paul and Silas were praying and singing hymns to God, and the prisoners were listening to them. 26 Suddenly there was a great earthquake, so*

that the foundations of the prison were shaken; and immediately all the doors were opened and everyone's chains were loosed.

- Acts 16:20-26

They were publicly stripped naked, beaten, thrown in prison, and after all that comes a *suddenly* moment? That sounds more like a *finally-you-showed-up-moment*! A *where-were-you-a-couple-hours-ago-moment*? But, get this, in every strike there's a moment of breakthrough, a moment of change, a *suddenly* moment. It is my observation that God loves turning our finallys into His suddenlys, and nothing will turn your finally into a suddenly any more than a season of prayer and fasting.

In what area of your life could God turn your finally into His suddenly? Just because it hasn't happened yet, doesn't mean it's not going to happen. Delay does not mean denial. In Jeremiah 32:27, God says, *"Behold, I am the LORD, the God of all flesh. Is there anything too hard for Me?"* Of course, the answer is a resounding "No!" Nothing is too hard for the Lord. If God managed to save the universe with a baby – a baby born to a teen mom, in an unsanitary environment, to a skeptical spouse who knew he wasn't the baby's father, then why would your situation be too difficult for Him?

Pay It Out or Pray It Out

GAINING SPIRITUAL LEVERAGE

The dreams God has placed in your heart can be obtained in one of two ways: you can pay for them or you can pray for them. You can pay it out or pray it out. In many cases, if you pray it out, you won't have to pay it out. We'll come back to that thought later.

Did you know there are 5,467 promises in the Bible? If you prayed through one promise a day, it would take fifteen years to pray through all the promises God's made to you. If you're a child of God, His favor is on your life. The problem is, we tend to believe more in karma than we do in the gospel. Karma says, "If you do bad, bad things happen to you." The gospel says, "You did bad, but while you were deep in sin, Christ died for you." The gospel says, *"He who knew no sin, became sin for you, so that you could become the righteousness of God in Him."*[2] The gospel is not about behavior modification; it is about life transformation. When you receive Christ, you receive a new identity. Before you received Christ, you were a child of wrath, born in sin. That's why you must be born again. Once you received Christ, you became a child of God, and God will fight for His children, and God's favor rests on His children. However, if you don't believe the favor of God is on your life, you won't live like the favor of God is on your life.

The other issue we struggle with is that we focus on the prayers that haven't been answered instead of those that have. We focus on the miracles that haven't happened instead of those that have. All of Israel's feasts in the Old Testament had one objective: to remind God's people of the miracles He had done, the prayers He had answered. The purpose of communion is remembering what Christ has done. Jesus said, *"As often as you do this, do it in remembrance of Me."*[3]

I am a dreamer, a visionary, and as I am writing this book, I am believing God for some incredible things. A few days ago, during my prayer time, I sensed the Holy Spirit say, "Make a prayer journal and make an answered prayer journal." If you don't remember the answered prayers, you'll forget that God answers prayers. If you forget He answers prayer, you'll give up before you see the answers to your prayers. When you look back at the prayers He has answered and the miracles that have happened, you then see the favor of God on your life.

As I journaled the miracles in my past, my faith began to rise. I recalled not long after we launched A Church Called Home, I was praying one morning over the church's finances. As I prayed, my phone rang several times. I returned the call after I finished praying. The caller was a gentleman who lived out of state and kept up with us online. He had won the lottery and wanted our mailing address, so he could send us a check. He tithed off his winnings! I said, "Brother, I've never encouraged or discouraged anyone to play the lottery, but since you played, and since you won, I hope it was the mega million." It wasn't.

Then there was the day a business man walked up to me at a coffee shop and said the Holy Spirit spoke to his heart to give me a check, and to tell me that God's favor was on my life. I had never met the man before.

On another occasion, someone gave the church a University of Tennessee NCCA Championship Football ring. We found a company online that purchased college championship rings. We sold the ring and deposited the money.

Years ago, when I was leading a non-profit that traveled to public schools, I had a dream of providing free prom dresses to young ladies who might not be able to afford one. One day, as our team prayed about that dream, someone called our office. It was a lady who owned a formal wear boutique; she had heard about our organization. She gave us over 100 brand new prom dresses. A few weeks later, another boutique gave us several new dresses as well. In total, we were given 130 prom dresses valued at over $30,000.

I'm telling you, there are two choices: pay for it or pray for it. It's been my experience, that if you will pray it out, you won't always have to pay it out. In Deuteronomy 6:11, God gave His people a promise. He said, *"I will give you large and beautiful cities which you did not build, houses full of all good things, which you did not purchase, wells you did not dig, vineyards and olive trees which you did not plant."* This promise was given to a people living under the Old Covenant. How much more should we be basking in God's favor under the New Covenant?

Melissa and I have a friend named Lisa who has an amazing testimony of the power of prayer. In April of 2011, she lost her home to foreclosure due to a series of back-to-back financial hardships.

She applied for a loan modification which would allow her to pay interest only, extending the life of her mortgage and thereby, avoiding foreclosure. Lenders do this all the time. But while her modification counselor was telling her everything was ok, the bank was foreclosing on her home behind her back.

Then one day, her bank informed her that her home had been sold back to Fannie Mae. Fannie Mae sent a real estate agent to inform her they would be putting her home on the market, and that they would pay her moving expenses if she moved out within seven days.

Shortly after the foreclosure, she heard a sermon on using the blood of Jesus as one of her weapons in spiritual warfare. She bought cranberry juice and olive oil, took them to church, and asked her pastor to agree with her in prayer that she would not lose her home. Then she mixed the ingredients in a spray bottle and sprayed the mixture around the perimeter of her home.

She declared that no one would ever be able to cross that blood line to evict her. She says, "I anointed my door posts with the mixture the same way that Moses instructed the children of Israel to anoint their homes on the night of Passover, and I commanded the devil to pass over my home and take the homes of those who serve him. I also reminded the Lord of His promise in Malachi 3:10-12 to bless me and to rebuke the devourer on my behalf because I am a tither. I kept a CD of the word of God playing in my home 24/7. I was desperate, and the Lord was my only hope."

One night while Lisa was praying, she asked the Holy Spirit to show her what else she needed to do to keep her home. Suddenly her eyes fell on a folded flyer in her purse; she pulled it out, unfolded it, and started to read it. The flyer was about a coalition of organizations that champion home ownership, and her bank was one of them. She wasted no time emailing a detailed account of her ordeal to the bank.

The next morning she checked her email, and one of the people she reached out to had replied. Her email had reached the highest level at the bank and the lady who replied to Lisa's email told her to expect a phone call. Sure enough, a lady from the bank called Lisa that afternoon, and told her the CEO's office had reviewed her case, and they would be giving the home back to her. One afternoon, Lisa heard a loud knock at her front door. It was the sheriff! After he drove off, Lisa and her sister went to check the mailbox and found an envelope from the court. As she read the contents of that envelope she began to tremble. The bank's attorney and Fannie Mae's attorney had sued one another in court. The letter said they would also purge all court records of all lawsuits and judgments as if they had never happened.

Lisa's new interest rate was cut by more than half of what it had been, and the new lower mortgage payment was now permanent! If that's not enough, that home is now a source of income for Lisa as a rental property. For the past seven years, she's been making money off what the enemy tried to steal from her.

The same God who moved on Lisa's behalf can move on yours. He is not a respecter of persons. He will do for one what He does for another. But it all starts with prayer and redefining what *is* and *is not* acceptable.

Have you heard the story about the little boy named Johnny who cried out to God in desperation? His mom was just as desperate. Johnny was constantly in trouble at school, and his mother was often called to meet with his teachers. Finally, in a moment of desperation, she made Johnny a deal. She said, "If you will be good for thirty days, I will buy you that new video game system you've been wanting, the one that costs over $300. It's yours if you will be good for thirty days."

Johnny jumped to his feet and shouted, "You have a deal, Mom! I promise I will be on my best behavior for the next thirty days!"

He went to his bedroom, shut the door, and began to pray. He knew this would require a miracle. He said, "Lord, would You please help me be good for the next thirty days?" He thought for a second and decided that someone as mean as he did not deserve such divine intervention. So he prayed again, "Lord, if

You would help me be good for twenty days, I'll work real hard the other ten." That still sounded like too much coming from someone as rotten as he. Once again, he adjusted his request, "Lord, would you help me the first ten days?"

Then he noticed a small ceramic statue of the Virgin Mary on his dresser; his family was Catholic. He grabbed the statue, and then a pillow from his bed. He stuffed Mary in the pillow, looked up toward heaven and said, "Jesus, if You ever want to see Your mother again, You better help me be good for thirty days!"

I love that story! You have to give Johnny props for trying. He was desperate. What are you desperate to see God do in your life?

George Washington's Prayer

By 1776 the colonists had declared their independence, but Britain was having nothing of it. British soldiers were arriving in mass numbers, and they were attempting to take control of New York. On the morning of August 22, 15,000 British troops landed on the southeast shore of Brooklyn. Without any opposition, they advanced mile by mile, acre by acre. The only resistance they faced was from a group of 8,000 untrained men led by General George Washington. In five days, the British troops surrounded Washington's men, and Washington's men ran out of gun powder. With the British men in front of them and the East River at their backs, nightfall came.

Washington decided to take one small boat and send his makeshift army two miles downriver to join a larger regiment of 12,000. One load at a time, all night long, they paddled up and down the river under the cover of night. A storm arose, and the noise of the wind and rain kept the British from hearing their escape. As the sun began to rise, Washington knew he needed several more hours to get his men out of sight, so he prayed.

As the sun broke over the horizon, there wasn't a single cloud in the sky. But then, out of nowhere, a thick dense fog rose up from the river and filled the trench where Washington's men were hiding. All morning that fog remained until the last man had escaped safely. That's just another example of the power of prayer. Nothing lies beyond the reach of prayer.

Elijah prayed, and fire fell from Heaven. One hundred and twenty people spent ten days in prayer, the church was born, and 3,000 were saved. Paul prayed, and the prison walls were shaken. Martin Luther prayed, and the gates of Rome shook. John Wesley prayed, and a great revival broke out in England. William Booth prayed, and the Salvation Army was born. Nothing lies beyond the reach of prayer. When we work, we work, but when we pray, God goes to work.

What are the areas in your life that need to be redefined? During your "hunger strike" what are you hoping to see change?

Chapter 5
PRAYER AND FASTING HEIGHTENS YOUR SENSITIVITY TO GOD'S VOICE

Have you ever known someone who seems to always be in the right place at the right time? Things just seem to always go their way. Is being in the right place at the right time a matter of chance or a matter of choice? To answer that question let's take a look at someone in Scripture by the name of Samuel. From his story, we learn several principles that will help us position ourselves in the right place at the right time.

First, let's consider what Samuel's resume looked like. Samuel was the last judge of Israel and the first of the prophets after Moses. Before there were kings among God's people, there were judges. There was no higher office than that of a judge. Samuel succeeded Eli as the high priest of Israel. He anointed and inaugurated Israel's first two kings: Saul and David. The Bible says that Samuel grew, and the Lord was with him, and He fulfilled everything Samuel prophesied.[1] I would call that a noble life, wouldn't you?

My question is, "Why Samuel? Did God just pick Samuel's name from a hat?" I don't think so. The answer is found in 1 Samuel 3, and that's where Samuel's story begins. In his story, we find a powerful lesson in positioning yourself in the right place at the right time.

> *The boy Samuel ministered before the LORD under Eli. In those days the word of the LORD was rare; there were not many visions. 2 One night, Eli, whose eyes were becoming so weak that he could barely see, was lying down in his usual place. 3 The lamp of God had not yet gone out, and Samuel was lying down in the house of the LORD, where the ark of God was. 4 Then the LORD called Samuel.*
>
> - 1 Samuel 3:1-5 – NIV

Did you notice where Samuel was when the Lord called to him? Samuel was lying in the house of God, near the ark of God. The ark was where God's presence resided. Notice this same passage from The Living Bible Translation.

> *Meanwhile little Samuel was helping the Lord by assisting Eli. Messages from the Lord were very rare in those days, 2-3 but one night after Eli had*

> *gone to bed (he was almost blind with age by now), and Samuel was sleeping in the Temple near the Ark, 4-5 the Lord called out, "Samuel! Samuel!"*

- 1 Samuel 3:1-4 – TLB

Samuel heard the call of God because he was close to the presence of God. Samuel had strategically positioned himself in the right place at the right time. When you're in the right place at the right time the right things happen. The opposite is true as well. Have you ever said, "I wasn't doing anything wrong. I was just in the wrong place at the wrong time?"

Some might ask, "Why doesn't God speak to me like He does to other people? Why don't I have incredible God stories like this person or that person?" According to Romans 2:11, God is not a respecter of persons. In other words, what He does for one, He will do for another. I like to say it this way, "God has favorites, and you can be one if you want to be."

Many times Jesus called out to the crowd saying, *"He who has an ear to hear, let him hear."* Jesus often used phrases like this to heighten an awareness to the reality of God's voice. He was inviting everyone to lean in, to get their ear in the right position to hear. Zacchaeus climbed a sycamore tree to see Jesus as He passed by. He strategically placed himself in the right place at the right time. A weak anemic lady pushed through a crowd to position herself in the right place at the right time for a miracle.

A blind man sat on the side of the road waiting for Jesus to come by. He put himself in the right place at the right time for a touch from God.

When we fast and pray, we are doing what Samuel did, what Zacchaeus did, and what many others in Scripture did. We are strategically placing ourselves in the right place at the right time, and when you're in the right place at the right time, the right things tend to happen.

The Stages of Fasting

Let's take a look at what happens mentally and physically when we fast. There are basically three stages of a liquid only fast.

Stage one is when your body transitions into fasting mode. It's by far, the most challenging part of the fast. This stage is where you start to feel the hunger pangs as you push away your plate. You suffer a loss of energy, and your head begins to ache. These effects lead to your being moody or irritable, so be prepared.

Several things happen at the cellular level that cause hunger and fatigue during this first stage. When you're eating regularly, your body breaks down glucose to get the energy it needs to function properly. While you're fasting, your body needs to produce sugar for energy, so it begins a process called gluconeogenesis. During gluconeogenesis, your liver converts non-carbohydrate materials like lactate, amino acids, and fats into glucose. As your body goes into "battery save mode," your basal metabolic rate, or BMR, becomes more efficient and uses less energy. This power saving process includes lowering your heart rate and blood pressure. At this stage, you may feel drained. However, if you stick it out a little longer, that lost energy will return.

Stage two starts around the end of day two and lasts until day seven. A lot of changes begin to happen at this stage, and you may start to notice changes in your physical appearance, as well as how you feel. Your complexion clears up, and you have a glow about you.

By stage two, ketosis has begun. Ketosis is a critical phase of the fast where your body starts to burn stored fat as its primary power source. As the processes of ketosis are carried out inside your body, you usually stop feeling hungry and tired.

Burning fat has several benefits for your health—the first being weight loss. Ketosis is a predictable way to target fat that otherwise remains untouched even with a healthy lifestyle. Getting rid of that extra fat has a detoxifying effect on the body. Your body's natural defenses use stored fat to hold toxic metals so they can't wreak havoc on your system. However, during ketosis, these toxic metals are safely expelled from your body as fat reserves get used up.

Stage three typically falls between day eight and fifteen. This stage includes dramatic improvements in mood and mental clarity.

By the third stage, a sort of "fasting high" begins. This boost happens when your body fully adjusts to fasting. While not everyone reaches this stage, those who do report a dramatic improvement in how they feel. These improvements include an elevated mood, increased energy levels, and a type of clear mindedness unique to fasting.

During stage three, your body starts to enter into a "healing mode." This healing process begins as your digestive system takes a rest from the common stressors and toxins it endures on a daily basis. Fasting also strengthens your immune system, encourages healthy aging and reduces health complications.[2]

The bottom line is fasting is good for the body; it clears the mind, and it quietens the soul. Nothing tunes your ear to the voice of God more than a season of prayer and fasting. Samuel heard the voice of God because he made a conscious decision to put himself in the right place at the right time. Being in the right place at the right time is not a matter of coincidence; it's a matter of choice. You can't catch fish without being close to the water. You can't hit a home-run sitting in the dugout. You can't land a godly man or woman looking in ungodly places. And if you want to encounter God, then choose today to be where He shows up; seek His face, be faithful to His house, and make yourself available.

Let me give you three tips to help you position yourself in the right place at the right time. Remember these three words: proximity, patience, and persistence.

Proximity – Where's your heart at?

Late one night, Samuel was hanging out near the ark. Late one night, King David was hanging out on the roof of his palace watching a woman bathing. Which of those two sounds more like you when no one is looking?

When God speaks, He speaks in a still small voice. He whispers. No form of communication is more intimate than a whisper. If you're going to hear a whisper, you have to be quiet, and you have to be close. You don't hear a whisper by accident. The goal of hearing God's voice isn't just hearing His voice; it's being close enough to His presence to hear Him whisper. The goal is intimacy. In the words of Mark Batterson, "Nothing has more potential to change your life like the whisper of God. Nothing will determine your destiny more than your ability to hear His voice. His whisper is gentle, but nothing is more powerful."

I've always been intrigued by Psalm 103:7. The verse reads, *"He made known His ways unto Moses, His acts unto the children of Israel."* In other words, the masses saw God do something, Moses experienced God do something. Have you ever watched God use someone else and thought, "Why not me Lord?" Sure you have. We've all done it. The truth is, God wants to do something spectacular in and through all of us.

Moses knew God's ways because he knew God's voice, and he knew God's voice because he spent time alone in God's presence. He was a worshiper, and he looked for God in unusual places. When God wanted to meet with His people, the people refused and told Moses, "You go up on the mountain and talk to God. You tell us what He wants from us and we'll do it."[3] On that mountain top, God and Moses talked face to face like friends. It's all about proximity.

Patience – Have you given up on a dream because it didn't happen in your timing?

I'm a car fanatic. A few years ago, our family was walking through the mall near our house. In the breezeway, a crowd gathered around a gorgeous new Cadillac. A local Cadillac dealer was giving the vehicle away in a contest that weekend. Here's how the contest worked: at a set time, anyone who wished to participate placed his or her hand on the vehicle. Once the contest began, if you took your hand off the car, you were out. Whoever had his or her hand on the vehicle the longest won. It was a test of patience.

Some dreams take time. It has been my experience that God is always on time, but He can be so last minute. Proverbs 24:10

says, *"If you faint in the day of adversity, your strength is small."* We are not people of little strength; we are people of great faith.

I heard a preacher tell a story about a girl named Sally who had been misbehaving at home and at school. One evening, her mother sent her to her room. Shortly thereafter, Sally emerged from her room and informed her mother that she had thought things over and even prayed about her situation. Her mother was very pleased by what she heard and encouraged her by saying, "If you ask God to help you to not misbehave, He will." Sally said, "Oh no, Mom. I didn't ask Him for that. I asked Him to give you more patience."

Notice the following verses on the subject of patience:

> *Rest in the Lord, and wait patiently for Him; do not fret because of him who prospers in his way, because of the man who brings wicked schemes to pass... For evildoers shall be cut off; but those who wait on the Lord, they shall inherit the earth.*
> - Psalm 37:7,9

> *I waited patiently for the Lord; and He inclined to me, and heard my cry. He also brought me up out of a horrible pit, out of the miry clay, and set*

my feet upon a rock, and established my steps. He has put a new song in my mouth – praise to our God; many will see it and fear, and will trust in the Lord.

- Psalm 40:1-3

By your patience you possess your soul.
- Luke 21:19

I would rather fail by trying any day than to fail by giving up. Be like the postage stamp; it succeeds by sticking to something until it gets there. If you've tried before and it didn't work out like you thought it would, keep working at it. Remember, even Jesus had to touch one blind man twice before he could see clearly.

Something else I've noticed over the years is that sometimes the right place at the right time often looks like the wrong place at the wrong time. But God can take what looks like the wrong place at the wrong time and turn it into the right place at the right time. Ask Daniel. I'm sure Daniel thought the lion's den was the wrong place at the wrong time. But God turned a lion's den into the right place at the right time to show Himself strong on Daniel's behalf. Ask the three Hebrew boys who were thrown in a fiery furnace. God turned that furnace into the right place at the right time for a miracle of biblical proportions. He can do the same for you. Be patient.

Shortly after we had launched A Church Called Home, I went to visit my parents in Alabama. The church was only a few months old, and my false expectations of what church planting would be like were getting the best of me. I was sitting on my parent's back patio, looking at the beautiful landscaping around their home. As I sat there, Mom said, "Did you know that every plant goes through three seasons?" At that moment, I knew this was not a casual conversation. She continued, "Each plant goes through a weeping season (when it looks as though you've failed), the creeping season (when you see a glimmer of progress), and the leaping season (when you rejoice for not giving up on what you planted)." That was such a great word at such a perfect time.

What season is your dream in right now?

Persistence – We celebrate fame; God celebrates faithfulness.

In Philippians 1:6, Paul instructs us to be confident in this one thing, *"He who began a good work in you will bring it to completion."* There are several important lessons we learn from this verse. The most crucial one is that God never quits, so neither should you. During the 1920s, there was a left-hander by the name of George Shuba who played seven seasons in the Majors for the Brooklyn Dodgers. They called him *Shotgun Shuba*, and his career included three World Series. His teammates said that when he swung a bat, it was like watching a bird take flight. However, his swing was natural for a reason - he made it that way. You see, George had a rope hanging from the ceiling in his house. He made knots in the rope where the strike zone was, and every day he swung his bat at that rope 600 times. He swung that bat 600 times a day until he made it to the Majors. That's how he got his great "natural swing." It's called hard work. It's called persistence.

I once overheard a man bragging about how much money his wife made in sales. Apparently, she worked around the clock. Someone asked the man what he did for a living. He replied, "I'm a go getter. I take her to work, then I *go get her*." That's awesome! We all have a hustle muscle. If you want to go far in life, you have to grow that muscle, stretch that muscle, and constantly push yourself. Have you heard the old cliché, "He who sweats the most, gets the most?" There's a lot of truth to that you know. At some point, you have to move forward, be persistent and stay after it. If you don't take action, you don't really believe in what you're praying for. Most prayers are only going to be answered when you act on them. Thomas Edison once said, "Opportunity is missed by most people because it is dressed in overalls and looks like hard work."

Learn from Florence Chadwick who gave up her swim from Catalina Island to the shoreline of California. She was only a few yards from the coastline, but a dense fog blinded her sight of the beach. Not realizing how close she was to reaching her goal, she gave up. Sometimes the difference between breaking down and breaking through, winning or losing, is that one last push when everything in you is screaming *stop!* Dead dreams die not because they were bad dreams but because someone gave up on them. In other words, don't put a period where God puts a comma. There's only one degree of difference between hot water and steam. Keep praying. In the words of John Mason, "With persistence the snail entered the ark."

God is Still Speaking

When I was in middle school, my parents built a beautiful yellow farm house on a piece of land once owned by my great grandparents. For years, I thought the house was haunted. Every night, when my family would drift off to sleep, our yellow house would come alive. The dishes in the cabinets, the pipes in the walls, and the boards behind the sheetrock would work together to create what could have been the soundtrack for the next Freddy Krueger movie. I just knew my great-grandmother was mad we tore down her outhouse.

As I got older I realized my house had been making noises all day. I just hadn't been still enough and quiet enough to hear it. And so it is in our faith. Two hundred and fifty times the Bible records the words, *"And the Lord spoke."* One thousand and thirty two times the Bible says, *"And the Lord said."*

The word of the Lord came to Jonah, *"Go to the great city of Nineveh and preach against it, because its wickedness has come up before Me."*[4]

The Lord said to Moses, *"I have indeed seen the misery of my people in Egypt. I have heard them crying out because of their slave drivers, and I am concerned about their suffering... So now, go. I am sending you to Pharaoh to bring my people the Israelites out of Egypt."*[5]

First comes instruction, then action. We tend to act first, and then ask God to bless our action. Everything begins with hearing the voice of God. Show me someone who's desperate to hear God's voice, and I'll show you someone who's soon to change the world.

Sometime back, I was reading through the book of Ezekiel. There's no telling how many times I've read that book of the Bible. However, this time, I noticed something I hadn't noticed before. Check out the following passage:

> *In my thirtieth year, in the fourth month on the fifth day, while I was among the exiles by the Kebar River, the heavens were opened and I saw visions of God. On the fifth of the month—it was the fifth year of the exile of King Jehoiachin—the word of the Lord came to Ezekiel the priest...*
> - Ezekiel 1:1-3

GAINING SPIRITUAL LEVERAGE

Notice he knew when it was, and where he was, when the Lord spoke to him. Now let's look at another passage.

> *In the sixth year, in the sixth month on the fifth day, while I was sitting in my house and the elders of Judah were sitting before me, the hand of the Sovereign Lord came on me there... 5 And He said to me...*
>
> - Ezekiel 8:1, 5

Once again, he knew when it was, and where he was, when the Lord spoke to him. Let me give you two more examples.

> *In the seventh year, in the fifth month on the tenth day, some of the elders of Israel came to inquire of the Lord, and they sat down in front of me. 2 Then the word of the Lord came to me...*
>
> - Ezekiel 20:1-2

> *In the ninth year, in the tenth month on the tenth day, the word of the Lord came to me...*
>
> - Ezekiel 24:1

We see statements like these 43 times throughout the book of Ezekiel. Each time, the prophet recalls with amazing detail, when it was, and where he was, when the Lord spoke to him. One of the most important things you and I could ever learn to do as God's children is to hear His voice. Everything begins with hearing His voice. In his book, *Hear God's Voice*, Derek Prince writes, "Nothing is more important to our spiritual life than learning to hear God's voice. We must take responsibility for making time not only to hear, but to test, what we hear spiritually. No one can do this for us. If you go on being as busy as you are, with little time for waiting on God to speak, you might jeopardize your future. We need to take time to hear God's voice."

In college, my major was art and design. During my final semester of undergrad, my pastor asked me to consider coming on staff as the church's youth pastor. My heart pounded for ministry, so this was an exciting opportunity, or so I thought. I asked my pastor what the salary would be. He said, "I'm not going to tell you that. First, you need to decide if this is something the Lord has called you to do." I was speechless. How could I make a decision without knowing the pay? Melissa and I were getting married that summer. My parents helped put me through college. I had to make a living for crying out loud! Then my pastor said, "If you make all your decisions based on a salary, you'll be running from place to place your entire life. You need to hear from God on this. Hearing from God enables you to lead with boldness, and once you've heard from the Lord, you can weather any storm that comes your way." At the time, I wanted to tell him to jump in the lake, but looking back, I value his wisdom greatly.

When you have a clear word from God, it gives you confidence moving forward. When times get tough, and they will, the difference between breakdown and breakthrough will be knowing you heard God's voice. When you know you heard His voice, you have the spiritual leverage needed to move beyond where you are to where you're destined to be.

I can take you to the place where the Lord spoke to me about launching A Church Called Home. I was praying with my dear friend, Pastor Randy Rice, at 6:00 am in West Chester, Ohio. We were in the sanctuary of the church he pastors. As I walked the back of that auditorium, God spoke to my heart to move from where my family and I lived at the time to launch the church we now pastor in Knoxville, Tennessee. That morning I left that sanctuary confident of our next step.

Nothing is as empowering as prayer. Nothing settles the nerves and brings more clarity than prayer. Jesus, knowing He was about to be betrayed, beaten and crucified, went off to the Garden of Gethsemane to pray. Not in our wildest dreams could we ever imagine the anxiety He felt that night in the garden. The pressure of what was to come was so great that His sweat became as drops of blood. But in that stress, something happened as He prayed.

Three times before His arrest, He slipped off into the night to pray. As Jesus prayed, we see a change in His vocabulary. Notice how His demeanor changed as He prayed. He went off to pray the first time and He said, *"If it is possible, may this cup be taken away from Me."[6]* Later that evening He prayed again and notice how His wording changed, *"If it is not possible for this cup to be taken away unless I drink it, may Your will be done."[7]*

He walked away from that second time of prayer and checked on the disciples. Finding them asleep, He woke them up, encouraged them to pray, then, off He went for a third time of prayer. Judas led a mob into the garden to arrest Jesus, Peter cut off a guy's ear, and what did Jesus say? With resolve in His voice, He said, *"Shall I not drink the cup the Father has given Me?"[8]*

Do you see the difference prayer made? As Jesus prayed, the Father's will became clearer. He walked into prayer unsure, *"Father if it is possible, may this cup be taken away..."* He walked out of prayer with clarity, *"Shall I not drink of the cup..."* He walked into prayer full of anxiety. He walked out of prayer with His nerves settled. Taking the time to pray can be the difference between a breakdown and a breakthrough. Jesus walked away from prayer confident and clear.

Being decisive hinges greatly on our ability to hear the voice of God. Indecision is deadly. Some of the most miserable people are those who can never make up their mind. Nothing lives long in the middle of the road. Live prayerfully, decisively, and confidently. Harry Truman once said, "Some questions cannot be answered, but they can be decided." When you hear from the Lord, even if you don't have all the facts you want, you will have enough to make a decision. I'm not suggesting that you live foolishly. God's voice sounds a lot like my wife's voice, if you know what I mean. If I think I've heard from God and she's not on board, I need to pray it through and be patient. Nevertheless, indecisiveness is not God's will. Consider the following verses:

In Him there is no shadow of turning.
- James 1:17

A double-minded man is unstable in all his ways.
- James 1:8

We are not of those who shrink back.
- Hebrews 10

Hearing God's voice gives you vision, direction, motivation, confidence and clarity. Joshua could invade thirty-one nations with a million slaves and possess the land of promise because he had a word from God. Think about that. What is the last word you received from the Lord? Write it down. Has it come to pass yet? Have you acted on it?

This might sound random, but did you know every zebra has its own unique pattern of stripes? No two zebras have the same striping. When a colt is born, its mother presses hard against her colt. For weeks, she circles her new born. She turns her body repeatedly pacing around and around her little one, clockwise then counter clockwise. Day after day she repeats the routine. Why? She wants her colt to know her stripes. After several weeks, the mother can be among hundreds of other zebras, and her colt can pick her out in an instant. Jesus said, *"My sheep, know My voice, and the voice of a stranger they will not follow, for they know not the voice of the stranger."*[9]

Even Jesus lived dependent on hearing the voice of the Heavenly Father. He said, *"I don't speak My own words, I speak what I hear the Father say." (John 12:49-50, 5:19, 8:28, 8:38* and *15:15)*. If Jesus needed to hear the voice of The Father, where does that leave us? He said that when the Holy Spirit comes, *"He will not speak on His own authority and He will only speak what He hears."*[10]

God is still speaking to people today. We just have to get still enough and quiet enough to hear His voice. This is why Scripture tells us to *be still and know that He is God*. Genesis 15 says, *"...and the word of the Lord came to Abraham..."* First Kings 13:20 says, *"Now it came to pass as they were eating that the word of the Lord came to the prophet..."* The Bible is filled with these examples. When we fast and pray, we quieten our soul and tune our ear to the sound of His voice. How desperate are you to hear the voice of God right now? Are you desperate enough to push your plate back? Job said, *"I desired Your word, more than I did my necessary food."*[11] Desperation creates motivation. Ask the Holy Spirit to increase your level of spiritual desperation. Regardless of the length of your fast, the spiritual leverage you gain during the fast will be worth the sacrifice.

Many years ago, someone asked the legendary NFL coach Tom Landry, "How many of your players have what it takes to be All Pro?" He answered, "If they play for me, they all do. But you're asking the wrong question. The right question is, 'Which of my players are willing to pay the price to be All Pro?' That's the real question." When you received Christ in your life, a world changer invaded your heart. There's a history maker living in you. A water walker lives inside you. Get desperate! Ask God for the impossible. Don't settle for mediocrity. Be All Pro or nothing. Dream audaciously, live fearlessly, and walk confidently.

One of the greatest leadership books I've read is a book by Samuel Chand entitled *Leadership Pain*. The premise of the book is that highly achieving people accomplish much, not because they are more gifted than others, but because they're willing to do what's necessary to succeed. They have a higher pain threshold. The truth is, if you're not hurting, you're not living. Pain is a part of the process. Most often, the difference between where I am and where I dream of being is the pain I'm unwilling to endure to get there. Pain is a gift. Ask any leper, and he will agree. Make a mental decision right now to refuse to die short of everything God called you to be. No more excuses! Excuses are for people who don't want it bad enough. You cannot make progress while making excuses. Don't live your life as if the goal is to arrive safely at death.

Chapter 6
THE SUN STOOD STILL

March 11, 2011, started out as a normal Friday for most people. By 3 o'clock that afternoon, it was a day many would never forget. Several miles off the coast of Japan, an earthquake registering 9.1 on the Richter scale created a wall of water thirty feet high. The tsunami moved inland at a speed of 497 mph. The average speed at which water moves during a flash flood is 10 mph. Water moving at a speed of 10 mph exerts the same amount of pressure as wind moving at a speed of 270 mph. Most tornadoes have a wind speed of around 100 mph. So, a wave of water moving at a speed of 497 mph is like a gust of wind moving at 13,419 mph. Keep in mind, the strongest wind ever recorded was captured by the Center for Severe Weather on May 3, 1999. That day, a passing tornado was recorded as having a windspeed of 301 mph.

When the tsunami hit the Japanese coast, the force was so great it permanently moved the coastline six feet. The wall of water reached six miles inland, and over 21,000 people were killed by the devastation. A quarter of a million properties were destroyed in the mayhem. Believe it or not, according to meteorologists the earthquake slowed the earth's rotation by one microsecond – that's one ten-thousandth of a second. That means for a fraction of a second, the sun stood still.

Change the scene to Joshua chapter 10. Joshua was leading Israel into battle. He and his men were in unfamiliar territory, and evening was fast approaching. Joshua knew if the sun set and darkness fell upon the battlefield, they would be at a grave disadvantage. At that moment, Joshua did the unthinkable. In the heat of the battle, he stopped to pray. Pointing his finger to the sky, he commanded the sun to stand still until they defeated their enemies. For twenty-four hours, the sun stood still.

The earth spins at a speed of 1,000 mph while circling the sun at a speed of 16,000 mph. However, in Joshua 10, everything stopped. What do we learn from all this? We learn that it takes an earthquake of mass destruction to slow the earth for one ten-thousandth of a second, but it only takes a child of God one second of prayer to stop it for a day.

Come on now!

What disaster or plot of the enemy could we stop if only we prayed?

What needs to stop in your life and in the world around you?

Make it a matter of prayer.

Watch God move for you as He did for Joshua.

The world is shaped by prayer or the lack thereof. God told Jeremiah that in his mouth lay the power to plant kingdoms and to uproot nations. Prayer is the arena where overcomers are produced, and prayer works even when you don't see it working. Someone once said, "God only has three answers for your prayers: yes, not yet, or I have something better in mind."

Our prayers are the greatest predictors of our future. Show me how you pray, and I will show you your future. God told Israel He would give them a land flowing with milk and honey, but when I read the story I realize that they had to fight and defeat thirty-one kings to get that land. That doesn't sound like a gift to me. Did God give it to them, or did they take it? Yes, and yes. They took it because God gave it to them. Those thirty-one kingdoms were more than able to crush them. Israel did not stand a chance on their own. However, because God had given them the land, they were able to take it. Psalm 44:3 says, *"For by their own sword they did not possess the land, and their own arm did not save them, but Your right hand and Your arm and the light of Your presence, for You favored them."*

Think about it this way. The state in which you live has a will. Your state highway department posts speed limit signs to indicate the will of the state. In some places the state says, "Do not exceed a speed of 55 mph." In other places, the limit is 25 mph. You get the idea. However, if there's no one employed to enforce the will of the state, we all know what happens.

Growing up, there was a stretch of highway where my friends and I drag raced. Don't judge me! We always raced there because we had never seen police there. Although the speed limit was 55 mph, we more than doubled that at times. You might not be out drag racing, nor do I these days, but I'm sure you often find yourself on a stretch of highway that has an unrealistic speed limit posted. If the police seldom venture there, chances are you do what everyone else does, you break the speed limit. The state doesn't get what the state wills, unless someone is present to enforce its will. If you are a Christ follower, you have been employed to enforce God's will. That's what you do when you pray. The day you received Christ, you were deputized by Heaven. You might not see a badge on your chest, but the Holy Spirit has placed a seal on your heart. You have the power to stop some things in your life. Jesus said, *"Behold I give you the power and authority to trample on serpents, and scorpions and over all the power of the enemy..."*[1] He said, *"I bestow upon you a kingdom, just as My Father bestowed one upon Me..."*[2]

In Genesis 15, Exodus 23 and Numbers 34, God gave His people the borders of the promise land. In great detail, He told them how far in each direction their new land was to reach. But then He told Joshua, *"Every place that the sole of your foot will tread upon I have given you, as I said to Moses."*[3]

What?

Wait a minute!

GAINING SPIRITUAL LEVERAGE

I thought the borders were already established...?

They were!

The victory had been established in Heaven; now someone had to walk it out here on earth. When a piece of property is transferred from one party to the next, the title work has to be notarized. A notary stamps his or her seal on the paperwork, making it legally binding. Joshua became the notary, and his footprint became Heaven's official seal. Remember this: whatever you pray over, you rule over! Where there is no prayer, there is no power. Prayer is the difference maker. Prayer engages God and brings Him into human affairs.

One of my favorite people in the Bible is the prophet Elijah. James 5:17-18 says of him, *"Elijah was a man with a nature like ours, and he prayed earnestly that it might not rain; and it did not rain on the earth for three years and six months. And he prayed again, and the sky poured rain, and the earth produced its fruit."* Pretty cool right? But here's the deal, he prayed seven times before the rain came, and the drought ended. In 1 Kings 18, the Lord told the prophet that the drought was over, and the rain was on its way. Elijah knew God needed someone on earth to partner with Him in prayer, and pray he did. But after praying, and praying, and praying; six prayers in, there still was no rain. However, Elijah did not relent. He knew that the breakthrough was coming. James reminds us that it is the *"effective fervent prayer of a righteous man that avails much."*[4]

There's a five-word phrase that appears 436 times throughout the Bible. The five words are: *"And it came to pass."* God is still bringing great things to pass today. Those dreams He placed in your heart, He will bring them to pass. Don't give up now. When you pray, something spectacular is taking place.

Prayer Is the Currency of Heaven

Every kingdom has a currency. A nation's currency is the means by which its citizens obtain what they need. In Europe, the euro is the currency of that land. In Brazil, it's the Brazilian real. In Canada, it's the Canadian dollar. The pound is the currency of Egypt. In Mexico, it's the peso. In Japan, it's the yen. In the United States, it's the American dollar.

As Christ followers, we're a part of a kingdom. Philippians 3:20 says that *our citizenship is in Heaven*. This kingdom, like every other kingdom, has a currency, and prayer is that currency. Prayer is the means by which we obtain the promises of God. We have access to the Father in prayer because of the finished work of Christ. Why else would Jesus encourage us to pray as often as He did? He did not teach His disciples how to preach, but He did teach them how to pray. Notice just a few of the many statements Jesus made about prayer:

> *Whatsoever you ask in prayer you shall receive.*
> – Matthew 21:22

GAINING SPIRITUAL LEVERAGE

Ask and it will be given to you, seek and you shall find, knock and it shall be opened to you.
— Luke 11:9

If you abide in Me and My word abides in you, ask what you will, and it will be given unto you.
— John 15:7

Until now you have asked for nothing in My name, ask and you shall receive, that your joy may be full.

— John 16:24

Prayer is the currency of Heaven. Somehow Joshua understood that. Growing up on the coattails of Moses, he watched God move when Moses prayed. He witnessed the Red Sea part, a rock spew out water, and manna fall from Heaven. When Moses went into the tent of meeting to seek the Lord, Joshua was there. If a situation is not serious enough to pray over, it's not serious enough to worry over.

We need to see prayer as an opportunity. During the late 80s and throughout the 90s, Blockbuster dominated the movie rental business. At their peak, they managed just over 9,000 stores nationwide. In 1997, a small startup company came on the scene. The company went by the name *Netflix*. The young company was struggling to gain traction, so its CEO offered to sell to Blockbuster for $50 million. Blockbuster said, "No."

Today, Netflix has over 247 million subscribers, and it's 1 of only 59 companies in the S&P 500 with a net worth of over $100 billion. Blockbuster missed an opportunity of a lifetime. In 2002, a company by the name of Redbox was born. Blockbuster was given an opportunity to purchase Redbox as well, but they declined. Today, Redbox has over 40,000 kiosks nationwide. Once again, Blockbuster missed a golden opportunity. Blockbuster went bankrupt in 2010.

Prayer is an opportunity of a lifetime. Nothing promises a greater return on investment than prayer. The angel Gabriel said to Mary, "*With God, all things are possible.*"[5] The prophet Jeremiah asked, "*Is anything too hard for the Lord?*" [6] When Jesus rose from the dead, the word *impossible* was deleted from the dictionary, so when you pray, pray big! Take the limits off!

When the time came for Abraham's son Isaac to take a wife, Abraham sent one of his servants to choose the bride to be. Abraham gave him some guidelines and sent him on his way. When the servant arrived at the place Abraham told him to go, he stopped by a well and prayed. Notice what happened as he prayed.

> He prayed, *"Lord, God of my master Abraham, make me successful today, and show kindness to my master Abraham. See, I am standing beside this spring, and the daughters of the townspeople are coming out to draw water. May it be that when I say to a young woman, 'Please let down your jar that I may have a drink,' and she says, 'Drink, and I'll water your camels too'—let her be the one you have chosen for your servant Isaac. By this I will know that you have shown kindness to my master. Before he had finished praying, Rebekah came out with her jar on her shoulder."*
>
> – Genesis 24:12-15

Did you catch it? Before he finished praying, Rebekah came out with her jar. When you pray, the answer is on its way. Something incredible happens when God's people begin to pray. There's no higher calling, a more noble cause, or a greater resource, than that of prayer. Only God can move mountains, and prayer moves God.

For forty-five years, my father-in-law has pastored the church he and his wife Mary started. For three decades, Lilly Maye Brock was a part of that congregation. Lilly Maye often shared a personal story that testifies of the power of prayer. She and her husband Hestle were raising their seven children when Hestle lost his job. They lived in a coal mining community in Southeastern Kentucky. For years Hestle worked for the state highway department, but in the mid 1930's he, along with many others, lost his job. Hestle tried for weeks to find steady work. One night, his wife Lilly Maye sat down at the kitchen table and wrote a letter to the President of the United States, Theodore Roosevelt. She wrote, "Mr. President, my husband is a hardworking man, and we have seven children. He was laid off when the state made some cutbacks. He has not been able to find a steady job since. If you could please help us, perhaps contact someone for us, or direct us to the right people, we would greatly appreciate it."

Two weeks later, they received a letter from the White House. The letter was from Eleanor Roosevelt. She wrote, "Mrs. Brock, my husband and I read your letter, and our hearts go out to you and your family. Tell your husband to return to his former place of employment. His job will be waiting for him when he returns. Thank you." When the president tells you to hire a man back, you hire the man back!

How many of us would think of writing the President and make a request like that? Honestly, if I did write the White House, I wouldn't expect a reply. Yet we have access to One greater than the President of the United States, and He promises a reply. He says, "*Call on Me, and I will answer you and show you great and mighty things you know not of.*" [7] Scripture could not be clearer, "*We have not because we ask not.*" [8] What are you asking for? God told Jeremiah that in his mouth was the power to uproot nations, and to build nations. Prayer shapes the world around us. If that's the case, what will your world look like tomorrow?

God longs to take us to places far beyond our wildest dreams. However, we need to understand what attracts His blessing. What attracts the touch of God can be summed up in one simple word: *desire*. We see an example of this in the story of two brothers, Esau and Jacob. These were the two sons of Isaac, the grandsons of Abraham. God had a special plan for this family. Esau was the oldest, which in that day meant several things. For starters, whatever the other siblings received as an inheritance, the oldest received double. There was a special blessing on the oldest son. It was the oldest son who carried on the family's legacy. What God began in Abraham, He continued in Isaac, and on down the line. But Esau didn't desire the things of God. If you talked about hunting, Esau's ears perked up. He could stay up all night talking about his last hunting trip, but he couldn't keep his eyes open in a prayer meeting. He would fall asleep in church, but if someone mentioned fishing, he was wide awake.

Jacob, on the other hand, longed for the blessing of God. He knew God had something special planned for his family, and he wanted to be a part of the action. Jacob didn't want to be left out. His heart burned for the things of God. Jacob had desire. He wanted what Abraham had. He wanted what his daddy Isaac had. He was hungry for God's touch on his life. One night, the angel of the Lord came walking through Jacob's camp. Can you imagine waking up one night and seeing an angel walking through your bedroom? With no hesitation, Jacob jumped on the angel's back and held on for dear life. He was desperate for God's touch.

Did God touch Jacob? Yes! But He did much more than that.

He rerouted the course of Jacob's life.

From that day forward, when God revealed Himself to a group of people, He would say, "I am the God of Abraham, Isaac and Jacob." Because of the birth order, He should have been known as the God of Abraham, Isaac and Esau. However, because of one man's desire, the destiny of an entire family was redirected. In the words of Jesus, "*My Father is not the God of the dead, but the God of the living.*"[9]

Are you spiritually alive today?

Are you hungry for the things of God?

Does your heart burn with desire to see God move in you and through you?

One of the things I love about Jacob's story is that he wasn't a perfect man. In times past, he had cheated his way to the top. He was known as a liar, a con man, and a manipulator. The devil will tell you that God can't use you because of this or that. The greatest battle ever fought was on a hill called Golgotha, which means "the place of the skull." The greatest war you will ever endure is in your head, "the place of the skull."

Let me stay on the topic of our inner thoughts for a moment. I once heard Pastor Craig Groeschel say, "Your life is a reflection of the thoughts you entertain. If you change the way you think, it will change your life." That's so true. You cannot have a negative life with a positive mind; it's impossible. The flip side is also true. You can't have a positive life with a negative mind.

I once heard a story about an eight-year-old boy who could've been the poster child for optimistic thinking. Standing in his backyard with a baseball bat and a ball, he looked to the sky and shouted, "I'm the best baseball player in the whole world."

Tossing the ball high into the air and waiting for just the right moment, he swung the bat with all his might.

Strike one!

He threw the bat to the ground, huffed and puffed for a moment, grabbed the bat, and once again he shouted, "I'm the best baseball player in the whole world." He tossed the ball, waited, and swung.

Strike two!

He couldn't believe it! After kicking the dirt and beating the ground, he took a deep breath and shouted, "I'm the best baseball player in the whole world!" For a third time, he tossed the ball high, leaned back and gave it his best swing.

Strike three!

He dropped the bat, shook his head and said, "Man, what a pitcher."

That's how winners think. Sometimes you're the greatest batter in the world. Sometimes you're the greatest pitcher in the world. At A Church Called Home we say, "Sometimes you win, and sometimes you learn." You never lose unless you quit. It's all about perspective. You will always win if you refuse to quit.

Silence those voices in your head. Win the war between your ears. Change the way you think, and it will change the way you pray. Change the way you pray, and it will change your life. Perhaps there's a little voice in your head whispering something like, "You'll never be what you could have been because of..." You finish the sentence. What lie about yourself is in your head right now? Maybe that little voice sounds like, "Because you've always been broke, you will always be broke. Because your marriage has always struggled, it will always struggle. Because you had that child out of wedlock, he will always give you trouble. Because you failed then, you can forget it now."

Romans 12:2 says, *"Don't be conformed to the pattern of this world, be transformed by the renewing of your mind."* Think of the word *"conformed"* as two words in one: conned and formed. Don't allow yourself to be conned by the devil and formed like the rest of the world. The key to transformation is renewing your mind with God's Word. Where the mind goes, the man follows. Our lives move in the direction of the thoughts we entertain. Believe you are who God says you are. Believe you can do what He says you can do, and pray that way.

In 1803, the British created a civil service position that required a man to stand on the cliffs of Dover with a spyglass. His duty was to be a lookout against invasion. He was to ring a bell if he saw Napoleon Bonaparte's army approaching. For 142 years, there was always someone at that post looking, watching for Napoleon and his men. The job wasn't eliminated until 1945. Napoleon died on May 5, 1821. For 124 years, British parliament wasted time and money looking for an enemy who could not harm them. We often do the same. Your enemy has been defeated. *No weapon formed against you can prosper.*[10] *If God be for you, it doesn't matter who's against you.*[11]

Heaven is Within Your Reach

Growing up, my parents always went big at Christmas. It was by far the most incredible time of the year. Our house should've made the cover of every home décor magazine on the market. As my brother and I got older, our parents started playing a game.

They would hide the most expensive gift and make us search for it. Now it was never that far away. It was always somewhere in the house, but we still had to make an effort to find it. That's the way God is. When Moses saw the burning bush, it was close enough to be seen, but far enough out of the way, to be out of the way. Moses had to take some time, interrupt his schedule, and *"turn aside to see this thing."*[12]

Many of the great things God has for us lie far enough out of our reach that it will require us interrupting our routine to obtain them, yet they're close enough that we can press through and retrieve them. This is what the Apostle Paul often referred to as *"laboring in prayer."*[13]

The most incredible things are waiting to be discovered. Words cannot express what great things the Lord has hidden within your reach. Jesus preached, *"The kingdom of Heaven is at hand."*[14] In other words, everything you could ever dream of is three feet in front of you. It's that close! The kingdom of Heaven is within your reach.

So go get it!

Leverage the power of prayer.

Make the sun stand still.

Chapter 7
WHAT TO EXPECT WHEN YOU PRAY

On March 30, 1863, in the heat of the Civil War, President Lincoln and Congress signed a proclamation calling on the American people to take one day, and go to their places of worship to fast and pray, asking God to end that terrible war. Two weeks later, the Civil War came to an end.

As Joseph Stalin worked tirelessly to bring communism to Russia, the believers in England called for a season of prayer and fasting. They asked God to move in a way that only He could move. Two weeks later, Stalin had a stroke and died.

The world is shaped by the prayers of the saints. In his book, *Shaping the World by Prayer and Fasting*, Derek Prince writes, "Scripture establishes the general principle that the presence of godly people in a community is a strategic move on God's part. Paul uses a metaphor to convey this truth: '*We are ambassadors for Christ.*' What are ambassadors? An ambassador is someone sent forth in an official capacity by a nation's government to represent that government in a foreign land. An ambassador's authority is not measured by his or her own personal abilities but is in direct proportion to the authority of the government he or she represents. Before one government declares war on another, it will withdraw its ambassadors from that land. While we are left on earth as Heaven's ambassadors, our presence guarantees a continuance of God's forbearance and mercy.

> Ephesians 2:4-6 says, *'But God rich in mercy for the great love He bore us, brought us to life with Christ even when we were dead in our sins; it is by His grace you are saved. And in union with Christ Jesus He raised us and enthroned us with Him in heavenly realms.'*

In this passage, believers are identified with Christ in three successive phases. First, we are *brought to life*, or *made alive*. We share in Christ's life. Second, we are *raised up*. Just as Christ was raised from the dead, so we share in His resurrection. Third, we are *enthroned in heavenly realms*. We share Christ's kingly authority. None of this is referred to in future tense. It's all stated in past tense, as something already accomplished.

In Revelation 1:5-6, we are declared *kings and priests*. As kings, we rule with Him. As priests, we share in His ministry of prayer and intercession. We must never separate these two functions from one another. If we are to rule as kings, we must serve as priests. The practice of our priestly ministry is the key to the exercise of our kingly authority. It's through prayer and intercession that we administer the authority that's ours in the name of Jesus." When we intercede we stand between the way things are and the way things should be. That's what it means to *stand in the gap*.

Prince continued to write, "God has vested us, His people on earth, with authority by which we may determine the destinies of nations and governments." Prayer is one of the greatest opportunities, one of the greatest privileges, and one of the greatest ministries available to all believers.

For the first twenty-five years of her life, Harriet Tubman was a slave in Maryland. She spent much of her time behind oxen, loading and unloading wood, and carrying heavy loads which gave her the endurance of an athlete. Harriet was often beaten. As a child, her owner hit her in the head with a heavy weight after she refused to restrain a field hand. She suffered severe trauma from the event experiencing headaches and seizures for the rest of her life. Soon afterwards she began praying for God to convert her owner.

> I groaned and prayed for the old master. "Oh Lord, convert master. Oh Lord, change the man's heart." Appeared I prayed all the time, about my work, about everything, I prayed, and I groaned to the Lord. I prayed for master till the first of March. He began bringing people to

> look at me in hopes of selling me. Then we heard that some of us were going to the chain-gang. They said I was going. At that point I changed my prayer. I began to pray, "Oh Lord, if you ain't never going to change that man's heart, kill him, Lord." Next thing I heard the old master was dead. – Harriet Tubman

On September 17, 1849, Harriet mounted a daring escape, traveling to Pennsylvania and on to freedom. But she couldn't escape the burden she felt for her enslaved family and friends. Harriet travelled silently and secretly, back and forth, escorting slaves to the north. Rewards for her capture ranged from $12,000 to $40,000. Yet her pursuers never caught her. They knew she was in their area when black men, women, and children began disappearing from their plantations. She was called The Black Moses, and her song, the song of the Underground Railroad, was… "Go down Moses, tell old pharaoh to let My people go." Harriet made nineteen trips back and forth from north to south. When asked how it was possible, she said, "Why it wasn't me. Twas the Lord." Harriet understood firsthand the power of prayer.

An interesting bit of science comes out of Duke University Medical Center, where a study found that, within a group of 150 cardiac patients who received post-operative treatment, the sub-group who also received intercessory prayer had the highest success rate. The fascinating thing about the study is that neither the researchers nor those being prayed for knew that these patients were being prayed for at all.[1] Prayer works!

In 1993, my wife was diagnosed with ulcerative colitis. She was a senior in high school. For the following six years, she complied with everything her doctor suggested. Yet her body quit responding to the medication, and her condition worsened. Her doctor suggested she take more drastic measures, but in doing so, he couldn't guarantee the results. Her weight had dropped to 87 pounds, and she had gone several weeks without eating solid foods. Although she wasn't taking much in, she was still having bowel movements several times a day, passing only blood and mucus. I know that's TMI, but it's important that you know the severity of her situation. When her doctor suggested an even more drastic measure, she drew a line in the sand, saying, "Either God will heal me, or I'm going to go be with Him."

Her doctor was kind but straight to the point. He said, "If God did heal, He did so in the Bible, but today He's given you physicians like me. He doesn't heal people now like He did back then." Her doctor gave her six weeks to live. He told her she would never graduate from nursing school, never get married, never have children, and never be a nurse. A few days later, he sent her a letter releasing her from his care claiming she had become a noncompliant patient. Nearly three decades have passed since then, and that letter sits framed on the dresser in our bedroom as a reminder that God answers prayer.

Fast forward thirteen years, and I'm at a high school graduation in Bell County, Kentucky. There were over two thousand people in attendance, and we were halfway through the ceremony. A lady sitting next to me elbowed me and pointed to a man in the top row of the section below us. He was slumped over as if asleep. We both noticed he had been like that for quite some time. She suggested I go check on him. Why? I have no idea. I'm not in the medical profession. I don't know why I complied; maybe it was to make the woman beside me shut up, but whatever the case, I got up and started making my way down to where the man was. About that time, the person to his left nudged him and he just folded over.

He was dead.

Pandemonium broke out, and the principal, who was at that moment calling graduates to the stage to receive their diplomas, stopped everything. He asked everyone to remain calm, there was a medical emergency, and could someone please call 911. Because of the way the seats were arranged, no one could get this man in a position to do CPR. He had to be picked up and carried to the gym floor. The entire time, I was at his side praying for him. Three times the person doing CPR said, "I have no vital signs." The vice principal, who was a local pastor, came over to join me in prayer; so did the truancy officer. For about fifteen minutes, the man doing CPR continued chest compressions, and we continued to pray. I remember saying, "Death, you have to go in Jesus name! God, breathe life into this man's body just like you breathed life into Adam's body the day You created him. Death, you were defeated, and you have to go, in the name of Jesus!"

When we said, "Amen," the man sat straight up, pushing away the one doing chest compressions. He looked around, confused and startled, as if he had been awakened from an afternoon nap. The entire place erupted with applause. Everyone assumed the doctor had resuscitated the man. I slipped out to my car, drove about ten miles up the road, pulled into a parking lot, and began to weep. It was obvious to me I had seen a dead man come back to life.

Two weeks later, my wife and I were eating at Ryan's Steakhouse in Middlesboro, Kentucky. A man came up to our table and asked, "Were you at the Bell County Graduation a couple weeks ago?"

I said, "I was."

He then asked, "Were you one of the men praying for the man who had died?"

I said, "I was."

He said that he was the doctor doing CPR that night. He went on to say that he had been a physician for decades, and had never witnessed anything like what happened that day. He said, "I know people think I revived that man; I did not! I did absolutely nothing to benefit that man. He was dead!" The man was flown to the University of Tennessee Hospital. All the tests confirmed there was nothing wrong with him. The doctor then said, "The man was dead, and he came back to life, just like something you would read in the Bible. Would you please find that man and tell him God raised him from the dead?"

At that point, my wife asked the doctor, "Do you remember me?" Then I was confused. I had no idea how she knew this doctor. Wouldn't you know it, he was the same doctor who thirteen years prior told my wife she had six weeks to live. The same doctor who said she wouldn't graduate from nursing school, have children, or hold down a job. He was talking to the woman he told would never get married, and her husband was the one who prayed over the man he watched come back to life! When the doctor put two and two together, he broke. I am telling you, there is power in prayer!

There's Nothing Too Small Nor Anything Too Big

Words can never do justice to the love God has for us. Let me show you something in Psalm 147. Verses three through five say,"*He heals the brokenhearted and binds up their wounds. He counts the number of the stars; He calls them all by name. Great is our Lord, and mighty in power, His understanding is infinite.*"

For starters, why do those three statements appear together? What relationship do those three statements have with one another?

1. He heals the brokenhearted and binds up their wounds.

2. He counts the number of the stars and calls them all by name.

3. Great is our Lord and mighty in power. His understanding is infinite.

It sounds like three random statements, but that's not the case. Nasa believes there are 200 billion stars in the Milky Way Galaxy and 10 trillion galaxies in the universe. If each of those galaxies have the same number of stars as our galaxy, then there are one octillion stars in the universe. That's 1 with 27 zeros behind it. To help you wrap your mind around that number, let's translate it into time:

1 thousand seconds = 16 minutes

1 million seconds = 11 days

1 billion seconds = 32 years

1 trillion seconds = 32,000 years

1 quadrillion seconds = 32 million years

1 quintillion seconds = 32 billion years

1 sextillion seconds = 32 trillion years

1 septillion seconds = 32 quadrillion years

1 octillion seconds = 32 quintillion years or 1 quadrillion centuries.

You're probably wondering where I'm going with this, so I'll get to the point. If God named a star every second, then it took Him 1 quadrillion centuries to name them all. That means billions and trillions of years before He spoke this universe into existence, He had already named each star and planned its spot in the universe. If He had all that figured out before time began, don't you think He has your world figured out too? Don't you think He knows what you need at this very moment?

Just about anything you need to know, you can find by a quick Google search. It's top secret as to how many servers Google has. The best guesstimators say it's somewhere around 900,000. Google can tell you a lot about a lot of things, but only God can tell you the number of hairs on your head.[2] He has counted your steps[3] and written your name in the palm of both His hands.[4] No detail is too small that He doesn't notice. No obstacle is too big that He cannot move it. Call on Him!

Our daughter Tori was somewhere around two and a half years old when we landed our first pet, a black lab pup. She was cute, full of life, and loved to chew everything in sight. We named her

Puddin. She was the blackest dog I had ever seen, yet underneath her chin she had a unique white streak.

Shortly after we got Puddin, someone drove through our neighborhood and stole all the dogs on our street. The rumor was the thief was selling them at a flea market an hour away. Whether that was true or not, we don't know, but one thing was for sure; Puddin was gone. Tori was heartbroken, so in an act of desperation, we got her and her baby brother a cat. A few weeks later, we were playing in the front yard when the cat spotted something across the road, and the chase was on. As our cat was crossing the street, he was hit by a passing car right in front of our eyes! It wasn't an instant kill though. He scurried under a nearby house dragging his back legs as he went. I crawled around the home calling out for at least an hour. I had to assume the cat had gone there to die. Once again, Tori was devastated. How much heartbreak can a kid bear before her third birthday?

My parents, being the loving folks they are, bought the kids a goldfish. Do you know the life expectancy of a goldfish? I'm sure the mortality rate is somewhere in the neighborhood of eight days. Sure enough, two weeks later, the fish was belly up. We provided it with a nice Christian burial in the backyard, along with a modest headstone and floral arrangement. Actually, we dug a shallow grave and dumped the fish in it.

A couple months later, as I was strolling Tori down our street to a nearby park, still thinking of her pets, she began singing, "Oh where, oh where, have all my pets gone? Oh where, oh where, could they be?"

Seriously! She just kept singing that song. Then she asked, "Daddy, if I pray, will Jesus bring me back my pets?"

What do you say to a question like that? You can't destroy a child's faith with a rational answer. Being the quick thinker that I am, I said, "Tori, I bet if you pray, Jesus will bring you some new pets." As the words came out of my mouth, my mind was calculating how much that miracle was going to cost me.

She responded, "I don't want new pets. I want my old pets back!" And with that she prayed.

Ok, so before I go on, let me say, if I were you, I would have a difficult time believing the rest of this story. However, what I am saying is true – no exaggeration. A few days later, I woke up to the sound of a barking dog outside our front door. Frustrated, I jumped out of bed and went to run the dog off. When I opened the door, I couldn't believe my eyes. It was Puddin! I'm telling you, that dog came back!

Later that week, a girl from across the street came over carrying a cat in her arms. She said, "A couple months back, I came home one night and heard a cat under my porch. I didn't know whose it was, but I took it to the vet and nursed it back to good health. My parents thought it might belong to you guys."

It was our cat!

I looked at Melissa and said, "I buried that goldfish. I dug a hole and put it in the ground. If that thing shows back up, I am out of here!"

I wish I could look you in the eye right now and tell you that God cares about everything you're facing this very moment. Zechariah 2:8 says, "*Anything that touches you, touches the apple of His eye.*" The first miracle Jesus performed was when the host of a wedding reception ran out of wine. The miracle of turning water to wine was not a life or death deal. It wasn't about saving a life; it was about saving face. It wasn't a healing thing; it was a humiliation thing. The point is, God cares about you and what you're going through.

So, what are you going through?

What difficulties are you facing?

In what way can a loving God with unlimited potential help you right now?

Getting Desperate

A common excuse we use for not developing a disciplined prayer life is making statements like, "I don't really know how to pray." The disciples tried to pull that one on Jesus when they said, "*Lord, teach us to pray.*" They had been casting out demons and healing the sick; don't tell me they didn't know how to pray!

It wasn't that they didn't know how to pray. They just needed an alibi for not doing it.

Let me be real with you for a minute. I believe everyone is an expert on the topic of prayer. Allow me to explain. Have you ever been cruising down the highway on a beautiful spring afternoon when the weather's just right? You start to drift off in thought. Then you realize you just passed a police car sitting idle on the side of the road. You look down to check your speed and realize you were driving 20 mph over the speed limit. Your heart starts racing. Your blood pressure rises. You look in your rearview mirror, and sure enough, those blue lights are coming fast! You know as well as I do, at that moment, you become an expert on the topic of prayer.

What do you need the Lord to do for you? The most difficult thing He could ever give has already been given, and that's Jesus. Anything and everything else is child's play. Is that not what we learn from Romans 8:32? The verse reads, *"He who did not spare His own Son, but gave Him up for us all - how will He not also, along with Him, graciously give us all things?"* God is not insulted by bold prayers. He's a big God who loves doing big things for His children.

So, what are you in need of?

What dream lays buried deep within your heart?

In what way do you long to see God move in your life right now?

Build an Altar

The Old Testament contains over four hundred references to the altar. Every great individual in Scripture had this one thing in common; each one built an altar.

Noah built an altar (Genesis 8:20).

Abraham built an altar (Genesis 12:7-8).

Moses built an altar (Exodus 17:15).

Gideon built an altar (Judges 6:24).

Samuel built an altar (1 Samuel 7:9-17).

King David built an altar (2 Samuel 24:25).

Solomon built an altar (2 Chronicles 4:1-19).

And so on, and so on.

What is an altar, and how does one go about building one? Throughout Scripture, altars were used most commonly as a memorial; they marked a place where God touched the one who built it. Therefore, an altar was a visible testimony that someone encountered God at that very spot. As recipients of the New Covenant, when we make an altar, we are staking a claim. In Exodus 17:14-16, Moses built an altar as a sign that God would grant His people victory over their enemies. Thus, the altar became symbolic of victory.

After God's people defeated the Philistines, the prophet Samuel built an altar and named it Ebenezer. The word "Ebenezer" means, "Hitherto has the Lord helped us." An altar reminds us of what God did and assures us that He will do it again. When God told Abraham that He would give him a land, Abraham built himself an altar. That altar forever testified to those passing by that God had touched his life, and that he would possess what had been promised to him. The Old Testament contains over 400 references to the altar.

During the Second Great Awakening, Charles Finney was radically converted. Finney was a lawyer by trade, but on December 30, 1823, he was licensed to preach. Early in his ministry, he preached throughout upstate New York. For three weeks he preached in the town of Antwerp. On his third Sunday there, an elderly gentleman asked if he would preach in a school-house one town over. Finney agreed. He later wrote, "I arose and left my lodging; and in order to get alone, where I could let out my voice as well as my heart, I went up into the woods at some distance from the village and continued for a considerable time in prayer." In short, he built an altar.

When he arrived, the school-house was so full he could hardly make his way to the pulpit. He preached on the story of Sodom and Gomorrah. His text was Genesis 19:14, "Get up, get out of this place; for the Lord will destroy this city!" He described the city of Sodom and its wicked inhabitants, and how the city faced the judgment of God. He spoke of a righteous man named Lot, who was grieved by their actions. As Finney preached, those present seemed angry and unreceptive. The more he preached, the more frustrated they became. All at once, a heavy conviction seemed to fall upon the crowd. The congregation began falling from their seats in every direction, and as they did they cried out for mercy. Nearly everyone was on their face pleading to be saved.

It wasn't until later that Finney realized the crowd's hostility when he began his message. Unbeknownst to him, the name of the town was Sodom and the old man who invited him to preach went by the name Lot.[7] Such are the experiences of those who build an altar.

My pastor, Ernest Brock, often told the story of something that happened to him at a place where he built an altar. He said, "One day while praying, the Holy Spirit showed me a house. He told me that I would find the house on the east side of Pineville, Kentucky. He instructed me to go there and preach a revival."

Pastor Brock went to his sister and her husband and told them what the Lord told him to do. Pineville, Kentucky is a small town about an hour's drive from where Pastor Brock lived. He had never seen this house before, but for the better part of a day, they searched for that house. To hear him tell the story, his sister and brother-in-law thought he "missed the Lord." Then, they turned a corner, and there it was! It was exactly as the Lord had shown him. Pastor Brock approached the front door, not sure what to say. A man opened the door, and Pastor Brock said, "This may sound a little odd, but the other day I was praying, and the Lord showed me this house, and He told me to come here and preach a revival."

The old man began to rejoice. "Come on in! Come right on in!" he said. He had gutted the front portion of his home. Pews filled the room, and a pulpit had been set in place. Billie Wilson owned the old log home. Mr. Wilson told Pastor Brock that sometime back, the Lord had told him to prepare his house for revival. "I did my part, and I've been waiting for the man of God to come do his," Mr. Wilson said.

My pastor preached that revival, and twenty-three people were saved. That was 1957, and some of those who came to know the Lord there are still pastoring today. Pastor Earnest Brock knew what it is like to leverage the power of prayer.

The Prayer of Jabez

The first nine chapters of 1 Chronicles is a genealogical record beginning with Adam and spanning several thousand years. There are 911 names mentioned and 25 nations on that list. However, there's one man who stands out from the rest. Out of all those mentioned, the Lord paused to highlight one – Jabez. All we know about Jabez is what we read in two verses of Scripture. From those two verses we learn that his mother named him in a time of anguish. The name *Jabez* means "sorrow." Words are a powerful thing. Overshadowing his life was a cloud of hopelessness and dread. But apparently, Jabez was a man of prayer. He prayed, and God moved. Here's what he prayed:

"Oh, that You would bless me and enlarge my territory! Let Your hand be with me, and keep me from harm so that I may not cause pain."[6]

Verse ten ends with, *"And God granted his request."*

Prayer can change the trajectory of your life. Build an altar, leverage God's love, and pray.

Chapter 8
SOME PRAYERS EARN COMPOUND INTEREST

Some prayers are answered before they finish leaving our lips; others seem to take a little longer. It takes faith to pray. It takes greater faith to continue praying when you haven't seen a change. However, as we pray, remember, delay does not mean denial, and I believe delayed prayers earn compound interest. Is that Scriptural? Zacharias and Elizabeth would say it is. Nine verses of the first chapter of Luke tells the story.

> *"There was in the days of Herod, the king of Judea, a certain priest named Zacharias, of the division of Abijah. His wife was of the daughters of Aaron, and her name was Elizabeth. And they were both righteous before God, walking in all the commandments and ordinances of the Lord blameless. But they had no child, because Elizabeth was barren, and they were both well advanced in years. So it was, that while he was serving as priest before God in the order of his division, according to the custom of the priesthood, his lot fell to burn*

> *incense when he went into the temple of the Lord. And the whole multitude of the people was praying outside at the hour of incense. Then an angel of the Lord appeared to him, standing on the right side of the altar of incense. And when Zacharias saw him, he was troubled, and fear fell upon him. But the angel said to him, 'Do not be afraid, Zacharias; your prayer is heard. Your wife Elizabeth will bear you a son, and you are to call him John.'"*

"Your prayer is heard," the angel said. What prayer was the angel talking about? Their prayer for a child, of course. But they were old now, so obviously, the angel is referring to the prayers the couple *used to pray*. The prayers they prayed when they were young and ready for children. But that time had passed. Those prayers were long forgotten. She was barren, and they were far too old for that now. Zacharias and Elizabeth had buried that dream. They stopped expecting that she would ever be expecting. However, those prayers from way back must have earned compound interest, because Zacharias and Elizabeth didn't just conceive a child; they conceived a prophet, and not just any prophet. Their son, heaven's response to their prayer, was none other than John the Baptist, the forerunner of the Messiah. Jesus said of John, *"No greater man was ever born of woman than John the Baptist."*[1] God looked a great way back on prayers long forgotten, and answered them with interest. Prayer works even when we don't see it working.

GAINING SPIRITUAL LEVERAGE

In Scripture, prayer is likened to childbirth.[2] No two pregnancies are ever the same. Some deliveries take longer than others. Some take days while others come quickly. But, it goes without saying that you don't stop pushing until you see the baby.

Prayers of faith are recorded in heaven and never forgotten. Prayers are eternal. In the book of Revelation, we read about an angel in heaven waving a sensor.[3] The sensor is filled with the prayers of the saints. Your prayers have not gone unheard. God knows them, He hears them, and He has not forgotten them. EM Bounds said, "Prayers always outlive the ones who prayed them."

At least twice a year, I get away for a few days to fast and pray. In 2008, while on a three-day prayer outing, the Holy Spirit placed a dream in my heart. The dream was to send young people in our area to college for free. The goal was to locate students who needed a break, who would not otherwise receive financial help, and underwrite their college expenses. At that time, I was traveling to public schools doing character education assemblies throughout our state, so I had an inroad with the school system, but how could I possibly pull off underwriting a student's education? The more I prayed, the clearer the plan became. Our team would launch a tour of school assemblies called *The Becoming,* and address the question, "What are you becoming?" Your dreams don't determine your destiny; your decisions determine your destiny. The decisions you make today determine the stories you tell tomorrow. The question is never, "What do you want to be?" The question is always, "What are you becoming?" Once the message was clear, we just needed to figure out how the scholarships fit into the event and where the funds would come from.

We created a criteria students had to meet, as well as an application and essay they would need to complete in order to qualify for the scholarship. Then we hosted a luncheon for the administrative staff of the fifteen high schools in our region. At the luncheon, I proposed a question, "If we gave one of your students a tuition free college scholarship, would you make our application and essay a senior writing requirement?" They gladly agreed. Next we needed to figure out where the money was going to come from. Several months later, I was sitting with the presidential staff of Lindsey Wilson College watching my prayers be answered with compound interest. When the Lord first spoke to my heart, I was hoping to get a community college to partner with us and offer at least one tuition free scholarship. I thought if we could get $25,000 in scholarships funneled to a student here and there, that would be amazing. God had bigger plans. God always has bigger plans. Whatever you're thinking, He's thinking bigger.

We agreed that Lindsey Wilson would receive an application from every senior at the fifteen participating schools. They would use those applications for recruiting students. The schools would narrow the applicants down to ten finalists.

Lindsey Wilson would send charter buses to each school to pick those finalists up and take them on a college road trip. Our team along with Lindsey Wilson would choose the winners from each school. That was the plan, and that's what we did.

Here's what it looked like in dollars: in three years, we awarded thirty-three students a full ride college scholarship valued at $125,000 each, which totaled over $4 million. And it all started with prayer, but not just the prayer I prayed in 2008. I first dreamed of traveling to those same schools in 1992. Sixteen years later, the Lord answered those prayers with compound interest. The best part is, they're still awarding scholarships today. EM Bounds was right; prayers do outlive the ones who prayed them. Prayer has no expiration date. I spent seventy-two hours in prayer, and seventeen years later, those three days are still bearing fruit. The escrow on prayer is incredible.

In their book, *Pivotal Prayer*, John Hull and Tim Elmore share an inspiring story which testifies of the long-term impact of prayer.

"His life's dream was to be a missionary, and it looked as though it was finally coming true. As the nervous young man sat in the mission agency's office, he assured the interviewer that he and his new bride were committed to working hard, managing their resources as good stewards, and sharing Christ with as many people as possible. His future looked bright.

Then, it all seemed to come crashing down. During their cross-cultural preparation, he and his wife realized she could never endure the rigors of life overseas. Her body was fragile and frail. If they went to Africa as planned, she would certainly die.

Confused and emotionally crushed, the young man returned home. His tragic tale continued as he failed to find a ministerial position. The first blow had left him devastated. This one left him depressed.

One night he awoke from his sleep feeling the weight of his failed dream. He began to wrestle with God over his calling. How could God call him to change the world and then close all the doors to ministry? It was during that time of prayer that God reminded him of his original commitment – to work hard, to manage his resources, and to share Christ with as many people as possible.

He decided to work for his dad, a dentist who had a small business on the side that produced juice for church communion services. He built the company into a large enterprise. In fact, you probably have purchased some of his juice. His name was Welch, and his grape juice is sold in supermarkets everywhere. Mr. Welch has not only given huge sums of money to world missions; he has impacted the world for Christ in a far greater way than if he had gone overseas himself." [4]

Delay does not mean denial, and delayed prayers earn compound interest. Over his lifetime, God answered his prayer in ways far beyond what he could've hoped for. He will do the same for you.

A few days ago, as I was reading through the book of Joshua, I saw something in the third chapter I hadn't noticed before. Let me lay the backdrop; Israel had lived in Egyptian bondage for 400 years. God brought them out with signs and wonders, and they left with all the wealth of Egypt. For forty years, they wandered through the wilderness, waiting to possess the land God promised them. Now the time had come for them to possess it; however, before they could take it, they would have to cross the Jordan River. Let's look at Joshua 3:14-16.

> *So, when the people broke camp to cross the Jordan, the priests carrying the ark of the covenant went ahead of them. Now the Jordan is at flood stage all during harvest. Yet as soon as the priests who carried the ark reached the Jordan and their feet touched the water's edge, the water from upstream stopped flowing. It piled up in a heap a great distance away, at a town called Adam...*

Did you notice they had to cross the Jordan during flood season? For centuries, God promised His people a special land, and of all the days He picked to give them that land, He chose a day when the Jordan was flooded. Sometimes God's timing stinks, doesn't it?

The Jordan is not a difficult body of water to cross. You can jump from one side to the other in some places. But in flood season, you're not getting through it. During flood season, the Jordan can reach a width of 1 mile and a depth of 150 feet. That sounds like terrible planning on God's part. However, God loves it when the odds aren't good. He's the God of the underdog. He wanted to do a miracle on behalf of His people, and He wants to do one for you as well. But you can't have a miracle until you're in a situation that demands one.

This was not the first time the children of Israel crossed a large body of water. Forty years prior, they crossed the Red Sea, but this miracle looked different. When they crossed the Red Sea, God parted the water before them. He heaped the water up on the left and on the right. He dried the ocean floor, and then they crossed. In other words, no one got wet. However, in Joshua chapter three, they got wet. The moment the priests stepped in the water, the river was cut off at the city called Adam. The city of Adam was twenty-two miles upstream. When the Jordan is in flood season, the water flows at 10 mph. If Adam was twenty-two miles upstream and the water was flowing at a speed of 10 mph, how long did it take for the miracle to catch up with them? If my math is right, it would have taken two hours and twenty minutes for them to see the full results of what God did when they stepped out, or perhaps I should say, "stepped in."

For two hours and twenty minutes, they were saying, "This isn't working! This isn't the way it happened at the Red Sea! Where is God? Joshua must be out of his mind!" I'm sure there was a committee formed to educate Joshua on how it was supposed to be done - how they did it in the old days.

Please understand, when God gives you a promise, He doesn't back away from it. He's not a man that He can lie.[5] He means what He says, and He says what He means. He is faithful to a thousand generations. His word will not return to Him void.[6] He watches over His word to perform it.[7] When God gives you a word, don't let go of it. Hang on to it with all your might. You might be neck deep fighting the current, but the answer to your prayers is on its way. Your miracle is only twenty-two miles upstream. You are going to make it. The miracle is going to catch up with you soon.

Heaven responds to prayer. John Wesley said, "God does nothing but answer prayer." Sometimes we see the response instantly. For Israel, the answer came two hours and twenty minutes later. Either way, your miracle is coming. What happened to their enemies will happen to yours. Joshua chapter five says, *"Now when all the Amorite kings west of the Jordan and all the Canaanite kings along the coast heard how the Lord had dried up the Jordan before the Israelites until they had crossed over, their hearts melted in fear and they no longer had the courage to face the Israelites."*

Do you remember when Abraham prayed for Sodom and Gomorrah? Those cities were about to experience the consequences for their sin. What's interesting to me is there was an eighty percent change in that situation from the time Abraham began praying until he stopped praying. He began with, "*If You find fifty righteous would you spare the city?*"[8] He ended with, *"If You find only ten righteous, would you spare the city for ten?"*[9] That's a change of eighty percent. I would propose Sodom and Gomorrah perished, not because of their sin, but because a man stopped praying. Every time he prayed, mercy was extended. This is why Samuel said to Israel, "*Be it far from me that I would sin against the Lord by ceasing to pray for you.*"[10]

Even though there was an eighty percent change in that situation, Abraham received one hundred percent of what he asked God for. He prayed five times, so that means every time he prayed, there was a twenty percent change. I don't know how many prayers are needed between you and your breakthrough. I do know sometimes we simply receive what God has for us, and other times, we take what He has for us. The kingdom of Heaven suffers violence, and the violent *"take it"* by force.[11]

Let's consider something else Scripture says about Abraham. Genesis 19:29, says that when Lot was in Sodom, *God remembered Abraham and spared Lot*. That sounds wrong doesn't it? Lot was the one in harm's way. Shouldn't the passage read something like, *"God saw the trouble Lot was facing, and He spared him?"* What had Abraham done that God remembered?

He prayed!

Abraham had been praying for his nephew Lot. Circumstances don't move God, prayer does. Those people you're praying for now will thank you for it one day. Don't stop!

Blind Bart

Do you remember the story of Blind Bartimaeus? His story is found in three of the four gospel books. Let's read the story from the book of Mark.

> *Now they came to Jericho. As He went out of Jericho with His disciples and a great multitude, blind Bartimaeus, the son of Timaeus, sat by the road begging. And when he heard that it was Jesus of Nazareth, he began to cry out and say, "Jesus, Son of David, have mercy on me!"*

> *Then many warned him to be quiet; but he cried out all the more, "Son of David, have mercy on me!" So Jesus stood still and commanded him to be called. Then they called the blind man, saying to him, "Be of good cheer. Rise, He is calling you." And throwing aside his garment, he rose and came to Jesus.*

So Jesus answered and said to him, "What do you want Me to do for you?" - Mark 10:46-51

There are three observations we can draw from this story:

1. There's always something or someone trying to keep us from crying out to Jesus.

2. When we cry out to Jesus, He listens.

3. Jesus wants us to verbalize what we want.

When the Lord appeared to King Solomon in 2 Chronicles 1:7, He said, *"Ask for whatever you want Me to give you."* The king needed to put words to the hopes in his heart. Just as the universe was formed by the words God spoke, so our world is shaped by the words we pray. In 1960, an evangelist by the name of R.W. Schambach was preaching a revival in Washington D.C. One day while walking the D.C. area, he stopped at a movie theater at 535 Eighth St SE. He felt prompted to pray over that property, so he did. Schambach prayed that God would turn that property into a thriving church. Forty-nine years later, that property became the location of National Community Church. National Community Church is a life-giving church with multiple campuses where thousands gather to worship each week. God responds to prayer.

James 4:8 says, *"Draw near to God and He will draw near to you."* Think about what God is saying in that one verse. If you take one step towards Him, He will take one step towards you. But here's the difference, your stride is about three feet; His stride crosses galaxies and spans the universe.

Chapter 9
WHY DIDN'T GOD ANSWER MY PRAYER?

Never question God! Have you ever heard someone say that? I know I have. Yet, there are nearly 3,300 questions in the Bible. There are 77 questions in two chapters of the book of Job alone. Jesus asked 307 questions throughout the four gospel books. The Bible is loaded with questions, and if you've ever questioned God, you're in good company. In his frustration Gideon asked, *"Pardon me, my Lord, but if You are with us, why has all this happened to us? And where are all the miracles our ancestors told us about?"*[1]

After losing everything he had, including his ten children, Job asked God, *"Why have You made me Your target? Why do good people suffer?"*[2]

The profit Habakkuk certainly wrestled with God over a series of questions. He wasn't an atheist, an agnostic, or a skeptic; he was a godly man, a man of faith, a profit. Yet Habakkuk asked God, *"Lord, how long will I call for help, and You do nothing? I cry out to You, yet You don't save?*[3] *Why do You tolerate wrongdoing? Why are You silent while the wicked swallow up the righteous? Where is justice?"*[4]

Let's not forget that on the cross, Jesus asked God the Father, *"My God, My God, why have You forsaken Me?"*[5]

Once again, if you've ever questioned God, you're in good company. One of the things I appreciate about the Bible is the stories contained in Scripture are not Instagram moments. The Bible is not a highlight reel focusing on the best moments of everyone's life. There are numerous examples of good people wrestling with God over what appeared to be unanswered prayers.

The beautiful thing about our faith is that it's based on relationship. Because of Christ, we can have a relationship with God. In what kind of relationship can someone not ask a question? In what kind of relationship can someone not and be real and honest? If you're in a relationship and you can't ask a question, that's not a relationship, that's a dictatorship. If God knows you carry the question in your heart, wouldn't He rather you ask the question than to pretend it's not there? I don't think God's offended by difficult questions. I think God's offended by fake.

David was a man after God's heart, yet throughout the book of Psalms, David wrestled with God over difficult questions.

Why do You hide in times of trouble?[6]

Will You forget me forever?[7]

How long will You hide Your face from me?[8]

How long will my enemy be exalted over me?[9]

A common denominator in the lives of many people throughout Scripture is a feeling of being forgotten by God. Jeremiah cried out to the Lord, *"Remember my afflictions."*[10] Samson raised his voice to Heaven and said, *"Remember me I pray, and strengthen me."*[11] In 1 Samuel 1:11, Hannah fell at the altar and cried out to God saying, *"Remember me, and do not forget Your maidservant, but give me a child, and I will give him to You all the days of his life."* Eight times throughout the book bearing his name, Nehemiah cried out, *"Remember me, oh God."* Even the thief on the cross said to the dying Messiah, *"Remember me..."*[12] All these people cried out *"remember me"* because they felt as though God had forgotten them.

Perhaps you've been there.

Perhaps you're there now.

I assure you; God has not forgotten you.

Shortly after my kids were born, I bought a journal for both of them. Once a month, I would write a paragraph or two in their journal. When they did something funny or cute, I wrote about it. When they took their first steps, I wrote about it. I used those journals to capture memories and to remind them of how much I love them. I knew the teenage years would come, and during those years, I knew there might come a time in which they doubted my love. It was during those teenage years, I gave them their journal.

God has gone to great lengths to prove His love for us. Psalm 56:8 says that *He has collected all our tears*. Somewhere in Heaven, there's an enormous storage facility filled with bottled tears. One of those bottles has your name on it, and every tear you've ever shed has been recorded and preserved. God loves you!

As we've learned, prayer can be powerful, but it can also be puzzling. During our time together, I've shared some great moments of answered prayers. But I would be misleading you if I told you that all my prayers were answered in the manner and time I hoped for. I've learned that prayer is just as much about changing you as it is changing your circumstances.

In the early 2,000s my aunt Julia was dying of cancer. Our family had been praying for her for some time. We stood on God's promises and believed she would be healed. One afternoon, I sensed God leading me to pray for her. She and my uncle lived about two hours away. I called my uncle and asked if I could come lay hands on her and pray. He gladly welcomed the prayer. Upon arriving, I reminded my aunt, and the cancer in her body, that by the stripes placed on the back of Jesus, we were declared healed. After reading some Scripture we prayed. A few weeks later she passed away.

When God doesn't answer a prayer in the way you hope for; don't stop praying. At the end of the day, we have a choice to make. We can be tormented by all the *why* questions. We can live stuck in the bitterness of what *did* or *didn't* happen, or we can choose to believe that God is fundamentally good even when life is not. We can trust that someday we will see everything from His perspective. In the meantime, we can cast all our cares on Him knowing He cares for us.[17]

Shortly after my aunt's passing, someone else reached out for prayer. Their daughter had collapsed from a brain aneurysm, and miraculously, she still had a pulse. We gathered in the hospital waiting room and prayed. She was given no hope of survival. The next morning, she woke up as if nothing had happened. A few days later, she was released from the hospital with no explanation other than a miracle.

Prayer works.

Even when you don't see it working, prayer works.

Just as the universe was formed by the words God spoke, so our world is shaped around the words we pray.

As you enter into a season of prayer and fasting, mark it down; incredible things will follow. As you begin pressing into the things of God, You will gain spiritual leverage you never dreamed existed. As Paul wrote, *"Your eyes have not yet seen, nor your ears heard, nor has it entered into your heart, the things God has prepared for you...But He reveals those things to us all by the Spirit, for the Spirit searches the deep things of God."*[18]

Let's go deeper.

This is your year.

Today is your day.

Leverage the power of prayer.

Thank you for joining me.

Your best days are just around the corner.

- Jason

MY TROPHY CASE OF ANSWERED PRAYERS

THE BOLD AND SPECIFIC PRAYERS I AM PRAYING RIGHT NOW

END NOTES

Introduction

1. Colossians 1:27

2. Job 42:3

3. Daniel 2:22

Chapter 1: Gaining Spiritual Leverage

1. 2 Corinthians 11:27

2. Mark Batterson, *Soul Print*, Multnomah Publishing 2011

3. Mark Batterson, *The Circle Maker*, Multnomah Publishing 2012

4. Larry Stockstill, *The Model Man*, Destiny Image 2015

Chapter 2: What is Biblical Fasting all About?

1. 1 Peter 5:5; James 4:6

2. Daniel 10:13

3. Daniel 10:10

4. Acts 14:23

5. Source: World Bank Development Indicators & Worldwatch Institute

6. Matthew 5:6

7. John Mason, Never Give Up, Revell Publishing Group 2017

8. John Maxwell, *Partners in Prayer*, Thomas Nelson 1996

Chapter 3: Going From Good, to Great, to Greater

1. Mark Batterson, Primal, Multnomah Publishing 2009

2. Mark Batterson, All In, Multnomah Publishing 2013, P. 68

3. Deuteronomy 28:13

4. Matthew 23:23, Luke 11:42

5. Quin Sierre, Miracles Happen When You Pray, Zondervan Publishing House 1997, P. 37-39

Chapter 4: A Church on Strike

1. Acts 2:1-2

2. 2 Corinthians 5:21

3. 1 Corinthians 11:25

Chapter 5: Prayer and Fasting Heightens Your Sensitivity to Hear God's Voice

1. 1 Samuel 3:19

2. The Goble Healing Center, Dr. Edward Group DC, NP, DACBN, DCBCN, DABFM. Last Updated on August 25, 2017 (This is such great info! I'm going to have to fast longer than 7 days to get to the best stage.)

3. Exodus 20:19

4. Jonah 1:2

5. Exodus 3:7-11

6. Matthew 26:39

7. Matthew 26:42

8. John 18:11

9. John 10:27

10. John 16:13

11. Job 23:12

Chapter 6: The Sun Stood Still

1. Luke 10:19

2. Luke 22:29

3. Joshua 1:3

4. James 5:16-17

5. Matthew 19:26

6. Jeremiah 32:27

7. Jeremiah 33:3

8. James 4:2-3

9. Matthew 22:32

10. Isaiah 54:17

11. Romans 8:31

12. Exodus 3:3-10

13. Colossians 4:12-13

14. Matthew 3:2, Matthew 4:17, Mark 1:15

Chapter 7: What to Expect When You Pray

1. *The Science and Psychology of Prayer*, a July 28, 2010 article in Psychology Today

2. Luke 12:7

3. Job 14:16

4. Isaiah 49:16

5. Robert J. Morgan, *100 Bible Verses That Made America*, Thomas Nelson Publishing, 2021

6. 1 Chronicles 4:10

7. Robert J. Morgan, *100 Bible Verses That Made America*, Thomas Nelson Publishing, 2021

Chapter 8: Some Prayers Earn Compound Interest

1. Matthew 11:11

2. Colossians 4:12-13

3. Revelation 8:3

4. John Hull and Tim Elmore, *Pivotal Prayer,* Thomas Nelson Publishing, 2002

5. Numbers 23:19

6. Isaiah 55:11

7. Jeremiah `1:12

8. Genesis 18:24-26

9. Genesis 18:32

10. 1 Samuel 12:23

11. Matthew 11:12

Chapter 9: Why Didn't God Answer My Prayer?

1. Judges 6:13

2. Job 7:20

3. Habakkuk 1:2

4. Habakkuk 1:2-17

5. Mark 27:46

6. Psalm 10:1

7. Psalm 13:1

8. Psalm 13:1

9. Psalm 13:2-6

10. Lamentations 3:19

11. Judges 16:28

12. Luke 23:42

13. 1 Peter 5:7

14. 1 Corinthians 2:9-10

15.

16.

ABOUT THE AUTHOR

Jason became a Christian at the age of 19. He has twenty-six years of pastoral experience serving on staff at four churches in the area of student ministry. In 2005, Jason founded a non-profit organization called Mirror-Mirror, Inc. The organization hosts events in public schools reaching tens of thousands of students across the country. Because of faithful sponsors, the organization has given over $4 million in college scholarships, and awarded students with over $14,000 in new clothing.

In 2012, the Creech Family, along with a team of others, launched A Church Called Home in Knoxville, TN. Today the church offers a variety of service options to accommodate its growing congregation. Jason is also the author of the following books: *Making a New Start, A Step Toward Order, God Has More*, and *Navigate*. He and his wife Melissa were married in 1996, and they have two wonderful adult children, Tori and Chaz.

AUTHOR CONTACT

Jason welcomes the opportunity to speak at churches, conferences, and various business settings. For more information, to schedule Jason to speak, or for coaching, please contact:

Jason Creech

jason@acch.us

A Church Called Home

865-643-8900

P.O. Box 14141

Knoxville, TN 37914

More Resources to Encourage You

GOD
But everything
HAS
He has for you
MORE
is outside your comfort

— Jason Creech

A STEP TOWARD ORDER
Where There is Order There Will Always be Increase

MAKING A NEW START

Order now at amazon.com

Made in the USA
Columbia, SC
12 January 2025